Getting Started

with

dBASE IV®

Wiley PC Companions

Stern/Stern: GETTING STARTED WITH STRUCTURED BASIC,
     Second Edition
Murphy: GETTING STARTED WITH DOS 5.0
Russakoff: GETTING STARTED WITH WINDOWS
Kronstadt/Sachs: DISCOVERING MICROSOFT WORKS 2.0
Murphy: GETTING STARTED WITH WORDPERFECT 4.2/5.0**
Murphy: GETTING STARTED WITH WORDPERFECT 5.1
Murphy/Potter: GETTING STARTED WITH LOTUS 1-2-3,
     RELEASE 2.2
Farrell: GETTING STARTED WITH LOTUS 1-2-3, RELEASE 2.3
Murphy: GETTING STARTED WITH QUATTRO**
Arnolds/Hammonds/Isham: GETTING STARTED WITH dBASE III
     PLUS**
Gaylord: GETTING STARTED WITH dBASE IV
Wiley: EXPLORING DOS, WORDPERFECT 5.1, LOTUS 1-2-3
     (RELEASE 2.2), AND dBASE III PLUS

** Educational version software available

Wiley Macintosh Companions

Abernethy, Nanney and Porter: EXPLORING MACINTOSH:
     Concepts In Visually Oriented Computing
Nanney, Porter and Abernethy: EXPLORING MICROSOFT WORKS
     2.0--Macintosh

Getting Started with dBASE IV®

Henry H. Gaylord III
Pace Computer Learning Center
Pace University

Babette Kronstadt
David Sachs
Consulting Editors
Pace Computer Learning Center
Pace University

John Wiley and Sons, Inc.
New York Chichester Brisbane Toronto Singapore

Trademark Acknowledgments:

dBASE IV is a registered trademark of Ashton-Tate Corporation
IBM is a registered trademark of International Business Machines
Corporation

ISBN 0-471-58616-1 (5.25 inch version)
ISBN 0-471-58615-3 (3.5 inch version)

Printed in the United States of America

10 9 8 7 6 5 4 3 2 1

CONTENTS

Preface ix

Getting Started with dBASE IV

Introduction

Hardware Needed **1**
Software Needed **1**
What is dBASE IV **1**
Versions of dBASE IV **2**
The dBASE IV Tutorial **2**
The Student Data Disk **3**
Loading the dBASE IV Software . . **3**
Using the ASSIST Mode **4**

Accessing the Menu Bar **5**
Identifying the Dot Prompt Mode . **5**
Identifying Additional Control
  Center Components **7**
Using the Function Keys **8**
Exiting dBASE IV from the Control
  Center **9**
Review Exercises **9**

Lesson 1 Creating a Database File

Defining the Components of a
  Database **11**
Using the Help Facility **12**
Setting the Default Drive **14**
Creating a Database File **15**
Adding a Description to the File . **19**
Adding Data to the Database with
  Append **20**
Viewing the Data Entries in Edit
  mode **23**

Viewing the Data Entries in
  Browse **24**
Closing a Database File **24**
Creating a Second Database
  File **25**
Making a Backup Copy of Your
  Database **26**
Adding a File to the Catalog **29**
Review Exercises **30**

Lesson 2 Editing and Searching a Database

Retrieving a File into Use in the
  ASSIST Mode **31**
Modifying the Structure of a
  Database **32**
Adding a Field to the Record
  Structure **32**
Modifying Field Length in the
  Record Structure **33**
Printing the Record Field
  Structure **34**

Using the Go To Record Option . **35**
Editing Record Contents **35**
Using Browse Mode to Append . **37**
Using Searching to Locate a
  Record to Edit **39**
Editing in Browse Mode **41**
Deleting Records and Files **42**
Deleting a Single Record **42**
Review Exercises **47**

Lesson 3 Querying a Database

Creating a Query **49**
Multiple Criteria in Queries **56**
AND Queries **56**

OR Queries **57**
Review Exercises **58**

Lesson 4 Organizing Database Files

Organizing Database Files **59**
Sorting on a Single Field **60**
Sorting on Multiple Fields **63**
Creating Indexes **64**
Indexing on the Database Design
Screen **65**

Creating an Index in Browse
Mode **67**
Switching Indexes **69**
Review Exercises **70**

Lesson 5 Update Queries

The Delete Query **71**
Removing a File from the
Catalog **75**

The Update Query **75**
The Condition Box **79**
Review Exercises **81**

Lesson 6 Printing Reports and Labels

Creating Reports **83**
Creating a Report Format **84**
Refining the Report Design **87**
Printing the Report **91**
Designing a Free Form Report
from a Query **91**

Placing a Calculated Field on the
Report **93**
Printing Labels **95**
Observing Filenames Related to a
Database **98**
Review Exercises **99**

Lesson 7 Introduction to Programming

Programming in dBASE IV **101**
Entering the Program Editor .. **101**
Creating Program
Documentation **102**
Setting Up the Program
Environment **103**
Retrieving a Data File **104**
Creating a Menu **104**
Entering the Active Parts of the
Program **106**

Exit Section **106**
Append Section **106**
Edit Section **107**
Pack Module **108**
Browse Module **108**
Print Report Section **109**
Reading Program Error
Messages **111**
Review Exercises **114**

Appendix A: Home Inventory Project

Lesson 1 .... **115**
Lesson 2 .... **116**
Lesson 3 .... **117**
Lesson 4 .... **117**

Lesson 5 .... **118**
Lesson 6 .... **118**
Lesson 7 .... **118**

Appendix B: Personal Checkbook Project

Lesson 1 .... **121**
Lesson 2 .... **122**
Lesson 3 .... **123**
Lesson 4 .... **123**

Lesson 5 .... **124**
Lesson 6 .... **125**
Lesson 7 .... **125**

Appendix C: Civic Club Project

Lesson 1 127
Lesson 2 128
Lesson 3 129
Lesson 4 129
Lesson 5 130
Lesson 6 131
Lesson 7 131

Appendix D: Personnel Project

Lesson 1 133
Lesson 2 134
Lesson 3 135
Lesson 4 135
Lesson 5 136
Lesson 6 136
Lesson 7 137

Index

Index 139

PREFACE

This tutorial provides step-by-step instructions on how to use dBASE IV to create, edit, and organize database files. The material is arranged so that the first six lessons take you through procedures using the ASSIST mode and its easily accessed menus. The last lesson introduces simple dBASE programming that will create a menu driven system to further streamline database operations.

After completing the first two lessons, you will be able to create a file, add records to the file, and revise the file's records. When you have completed the essential part of the tutorial, the first six lessons, you should be able to satisfy all of your file management needs. The projects in the appendices as well as the review exercises at the end of each lesson provide ample opportunity to use the commands and procedures introduced in these lessons. However, because these commands and procedures are basic to using dBASE IV, you might consider completing each of these lessons twice to make sure you are thoroughly acquainted with the operations.

Lesson 7 will teach you to write a simple dBASE program that contains frequently used commands. Putting these commands in a program will save you from repeatedly having to select menu choices and will allow you to append, sort, and delete records quickly and easily.

Once you have learned to use dBASE IV to manage your files, to add, change, and delete information, to sort and index records, to create and print reports and labels, you will wonder how offices ever managed without it. Record keeping has never been easier!

ACKNOWLEDGEMENTS

I wish to thank Sally Arnold, Eleonore Hammonds, and Mark Isham, the authors of "Getting Started with dBASE III PLUS, Extended," the predecessor and foundation of this work. Their earlier planning and implementation greatly eased the production of this book.

Lynn Bacon deserves enormous thanks for testing and correcting the material included herein. Her diligence and discerning eye discovered and dispelled most of my errors, both large and small.

Also needing thanks are Nina Russakoff and Linda Carthew for their work on the formatting and index, as well as Babette Kronstadt and David Sachs whose sound suggestions and enthusiastic guidance eased the murky segments of the journey toward this work's conclusion.

I

Introduction

Hardware Needed

- IBM PC/AT/XT/PS2 or compatible microcomputer with 640K of memory
- Hard drive with one floppy-disk drive
- A printer (for some exercises)

Software Needed

- PC-DOS or MS-DOS 2.0 or later version
- dBASE IV
- Student data disk (for reference only)
- Formatted disk for use as work disk

What is dBASE IV?

A DBMS or database management system such as dBASE IV allows you to add, delete, change, sort, search for, and calculate information. Your college or university may use a DBMS to store information about you and your courses on a computer.

The information in a database is stored in database files, much as it would be stored in file folders. The files are stored on disks, much like file folders in filing cabinets. dBASE IV allows you to enter and use the information in your database file just as you would data in file folders. In addition, the computer quickly performs searches, sorts, calculations, and reports on this stored information. This tutorial contains examples of databases that could be used by many large and small businesses in their day-to-day operations.

The many uses or applications for dBASE IV include

- Mailing lists
- Accounting
- Scientific research
- Business information

▶ Personal use
▶ Library and government databases

Versions of dBASE IV

There are currently three versions of dBASE IV. The original release was Version 1.0, which was notorious for problems in handling many common operations. A fixed and slightly improved release, dBASE IV Version 1.1, replaced it about a year later. Still later, additional improvements were added and dBASE IV Version 1.5 was released. There are very minor differences on a few screens, and an occasional additional menu item in Version 1.5.

The illustrations in this book are from Version 1.1. The text has been tested using both Version 1.1 and 1.5. Since any new items in Version 1.5 are additional, they in no way affect the operations presented in this tutorial.

The dBASE IV Tutorial

This tutorial will take you through the basic dBASE IV operations using the ASSIST mode. As you complete the lessons in this tutorial, you may find that you will need to repeat some of the exercises in order to fully master each command and concept. Most of the commands and procedures you learn will allow you to create databases, enter data, store, retrieve, and/or manipulate this database information.

To use this tutorial, you will work with dBASE IV on drive C (C:\). That way, you will use your student data disk in drive A (A:\), and you will always save to drive A to avoid confusion. Keep this "save to A" distinction in mind as you work through this tutorial. If you have any difficulty in running the database program or finding your database data, you should check to see that you are on the appropriate disk drive.

Before you begin to create databases and store data in them, remember that the information exists only in the computer's memory until it is saved to a disk. While dBASE IV often saves data to a disk automatically, if you want to be certain to save all of your information permanently, you must exit from dBASE IV properly. If you fail to follow the necessary steps for exiting, you may be forced to repeat some or all of a lesson in order to complete the work.

This tutorial is designed to let you try several steps or procedures, then stop and review. To facilitate this process, each lesson provides review questions to allow you to check your grasp of the material presented in that lesson.

The commands in this tutorial adhere to the following format: All entries that you are to make are given in **BOLDFACE CAPITAL** letters. To enhance the appearance of alphabetic data, we recommend that you keep the [CapsLock] key locked in uppercase, unless you specifically want lowercase text.

This tutorial will take you through the basic dBASE IV operations, beginning with information on how to start your database program. (You should already have learned how to start your computer. If you are unsure about the proper procedures to turn on your system, you should review the GETTING STARTED WITH: MS-DOS tutorial before beginning this tutorial.)

In the early lessons, you will learn to use the ASSIST mode. In the ASSIST mode, you will choose from menu instructions for creating files, entering data, and using those data in specific ways. As you develop a greater understanding and ability in using the dBASE IV software, you will begin to use programming commands, which will allow you to be more efficient in organizing and executing frequent dBASE IV operations.

The tutorial is divided into the following seven lessons:

1. Creating a database
2. Editing and searching a database
3. Querying a database
4. Organizing a database
5. Operational queries
6. Creating reports and labels
7. Learning the basics of programming

You can use the dBASE IV software effectively without knowing or using its full capabilities and possibilities. Therefore, you will begin to learn how to use the ASSIST mode and complete quite a lot of information processing before you learn commands or programming.

The Student Data Disk

Packaged with this tutorial is a student data disk. This disk contains all of the database and index files that you will be creating as you work through this tutorial. Do not use this disk when you create your files. If you do, you will not be able to create the files correctly. Instead, use this disk as a reference tool only. For example, if you have created a database file and you do not get the correct listing of data during a search, compare your database file with the one of the same name on the student data disk; this comparison should show you where you have made an error. In this way, the student data disk contains the "answers" to this tutorial. Use it for reference purposes only.

Loading the dBASE IV Software

Follow the five steps below for running dBASE IV on a hard disk drive computer.

1. Turn on the computer and go to the C:\> prompt.

2. Check that dBASE IV is installed on your hard disk. If it is not installed, refer to the installation instructions that came with the dBASE IV software.
3. Insert your formatted work disk in drive A and close the door.
4. Type **DBASE** at the C:\> prompt (or the prompt for whichever subdirectory holds the dBASE IV program).
5. Press the **[Enter]** key.

You are now ready to begin using dBASE IV.

Note: dBASE IV cannot be run from floppy disks; it must reside on a hard disk.

Using the ASSIST Mode

When you enter dBASE IV, you are automatically placed in the ASSIST mode, and you will see the Control Center (as shown in Figure I-l). The Control Center organizes the display for easy access to dBASE IV's various operations. There are six main parts to the screen (as named in Figure I-1).

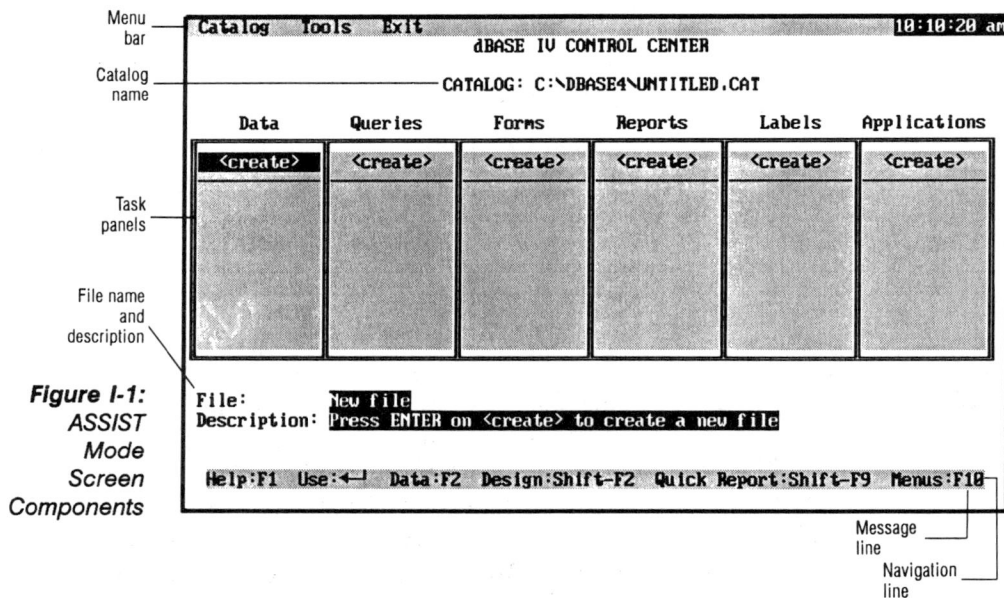

Figure I-1: ASSIST Mode Screen Components

1. **Menu Bar.** The menu bar in the Control Center consists of the three menus; Catalog, Tools, and Exit. Accessing the menus is described below.
2. **Catalog Name.** A catalog keeps track of all associated files for one group of information. You might keep one catalog for data and reports concerning your personal inventory, and a separate one for the school band. When dBASE IV does not find a previously created catalog, it creates one named UNTITLED.CAT.

3. **Task Panels.** The six Task Panels will contain the filenames of any Databases, Queries, Forms, Report designs, Label designs, or Applications (programs) that you create.

4. **Current Filename and Description.** When the highlight bar in a task panel is on top of a filename, that name and the file description that you have given to that file will be displayed.

5. **Navigation Line.** The next to bottom screen line lists some helpful keys that apply to the current operation.

6. **Message Line.** The bottom screen line lists instructions, suggestions, or descriptions for the current operation.

Accessing the Menu Bar

You can access a menu by pressing the **[Alt]** key together with the first (capitalized) letter of the desired menu. For example, the Catalog menu in the Control Center could be opened by pressing **[Alt]-[C]**. Also, the **[F10]** key will open the menu bar (but not a specific name.) A pull-down menu that contains specific action options will appear.

To change menus, you may press the **[Alt]** key together with another first letter or use the left arrow [←] or right arrow [→] keys to move to an adjacent menu.

Once a menu is open, you press the initial letter (without **[Alt]**) of the desired choice within that menu. A slower method is to use the up arrow [↑] and down arrow [↓] keys to move the highlight bar onto the desired choice and then press **[Enter]** to select it.

Some menu selections may be dim; those cannot be picked until the prerequisites are established. For example, you cannot choose "Remove highlighted file from catalog" unless some filename is highlighted.

If there are additional choices of action, additional pop-up menus, called submenus, will appear. The pop-up menu approach provided in the ASSIST mode should permit you to achieve your specific goals with minimal effort.

An open menu can be closed by pressing the **[Esc]** key.

The alternative to the ASSIST mode is the Command mode, better known as the Dot Prompt mode because a single dot or period on the screen prompts you to type in commands. If you press the **[Esc]** key while in the Control Center when no menu is open, dBASE IV will ask "Are you sure you want to abandon operation?" Picking "Yes" will go immediately to the Dot Prompt mode. Whenever you wish, you can easily move back to the ASSIST mode by typing ASSIST at the dot and pressing **[Enter]**, or by pressing **[F2]**.

Identifying the Dot Prompt Mode

The Dot Prompt has been retained in dBASE IV to keep it compatible with older versions of dBASE. The Dot Prompt mode is command-line oriented, meaning that you type in commands when you are at the dot prompt. When you enter the Dot Prompt mode from the ASSIST mode (by pressing **[Esc]** and pressing a Y to answer Yes), you will see a screen like the one shown in Figure I-2.

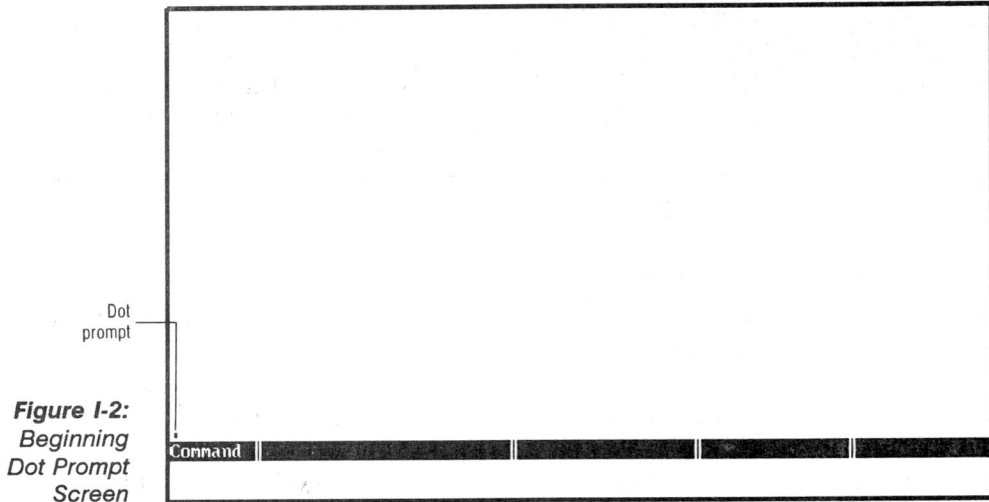

Dot
prompt

Figure I-2:
Beginning
Dot Prompt
Screen

Command

Rarely, if ever, do you need to visit the Dot Prompt. However, the Dot Prompt mode gives you access to a few commands unavailable in ASSIST mode. Also, entering commands occasionally allows you to perform some actions faster than selecting from menus. You can also place Dot Prompt commands together in a program that will allow you to perform complicated, user-defined applications.

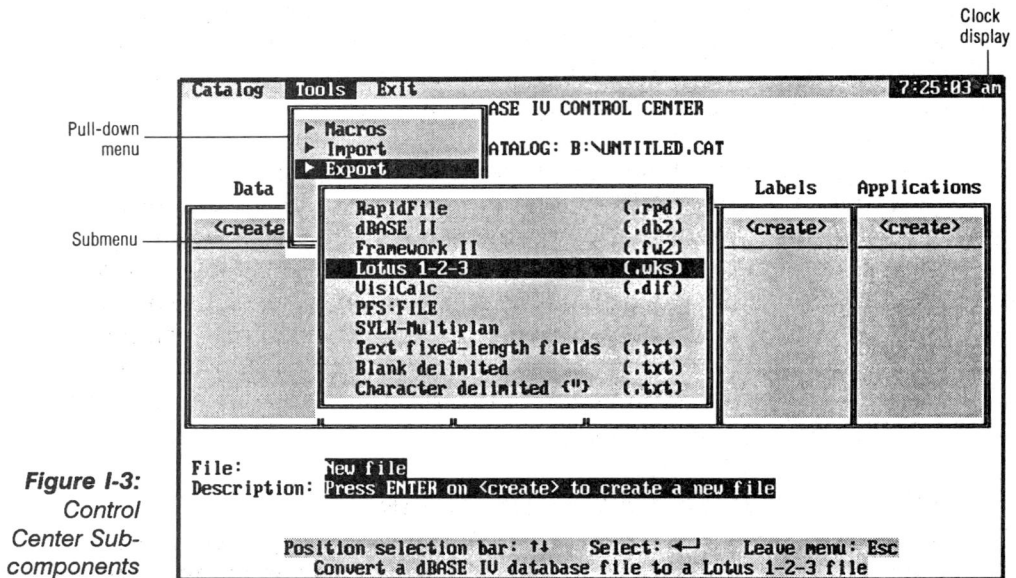

Clock
display

Pull-down
menu

Submenu

Figure I-3:
Control
Center Sub-
components

Catalog   Tools   Exit   7:25:03 am

    ► Macros   ASE IV CONTROL CENTER
    ► Import   ATALOG: B:\UNTITLED.CAT
    ► Export

Data   Labels   Applications

         RapidFile   (.rpd)
<create   dBASE II   (.db2)   <create>   <create>
         Framework II   (.fw2)
         Lotus 1-2-3   (.wks)
         VisiCalc   (.dif)
         PFS:FILE
         SYLK-Multiplan
         Text fixed-length fields   (.txt)
         Blank delimited   (.txt)
         Character delimited {"}   (.txt)

File: New file
Description: Press ENTER on <create> to create a new file

Position selection bar: ↑↓   Select: ↵   Leave menu: Esc
Convert a dBASE IV database file to a Lotus 1-2-3 file

Identifying Additional Control Center Components

The Control Center will at times contain one or more of the following subcomponents (as shown in Figure I-3):

1. **Pull-down Menu.** A pull-down menu offers a list of choices (commands) within a particular menu. For example, if you open the Tools menu in the Control Center, you will get a pull-down menu that offers the choices Macros, Import, Export, DOS utilities, Protect data, and Settings.

2. **Submenu.** A submenu is a secondary pop-up menu that contains further choices under a command. Some pop-up menu choices have their own submenus. To go to a submenu, type the initial letter of the desired choice, or use the up arrow [↑] or down arrow [↓] key to move the highlight bar, and press **[Enter]**.

3. **Clock Display.** The clock display, located in the upper right-hand corner of the screen, gives the current time. If your computer has a battery-powered clock, or you have set the time in DOS, the correct time will appear. Otherwise, the clock will have been initially set to midnight.

4. **Status Bar.** On nearly every other screen except the Control Center, there is a Status Bar. The status bar, shown in Figure I-4, contains five sections that display information about the current status of the program. The status bar's five sections are:

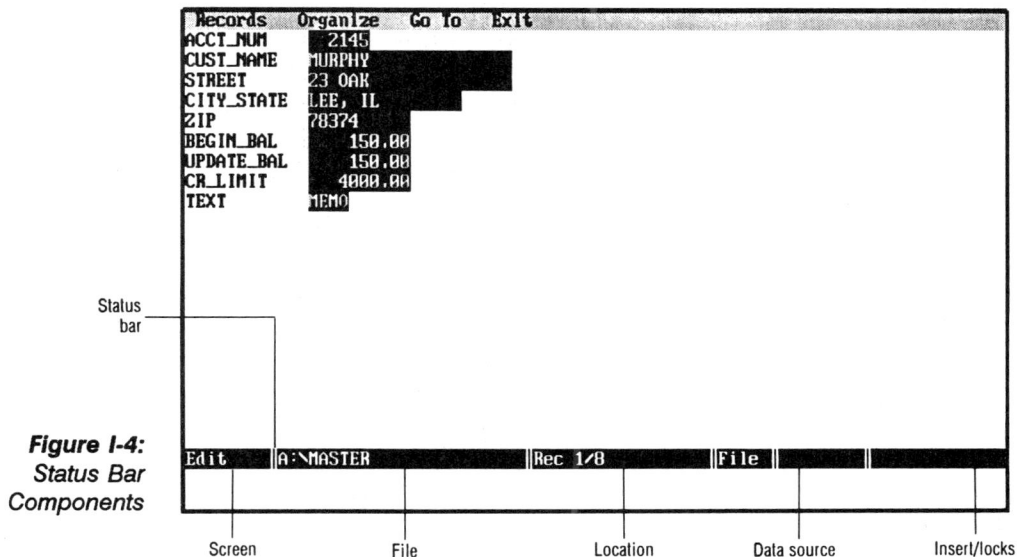

Figure I-4:
Status Bar
Components

A.   **Screen** shows the current screen name, which will be one of the following: Edit, Browse, Database, Query, Form, Report, Label, Program, or Command.

B.   **File** indicates the name of the file currently being modified. This could be a database, query, form design, report design, label design, or application (program).

C.   **Location** gives the position of the cursor. Examples include the current record number and total number of records when viewing a database file or the current line and column position of the cursor when designing a report.

D.   **Data Source** lists the database file that is supplying the data while you are working on a design screen.

E.   **Insert/Locks** indicates whether you are typing data in the insert mode ("Ins") or in the overtype mode (no indicator), and whether you have activated the CapsLock or NumLock keys.

Using the Function Keys

The function keys are located either on the left side of the main keyboard or across the top of the keyboard. The function keys are named with an F preceding the numbers 1 through 10. (If your keyboard has F11 and F12, they are ignored by dBASE IV.) The Shift key is also used in conjunction with the function keys to initiate additional actions.

In ASSIST mode these keys activate the actions listed below. Do not press them now. We will use them extensively in the following chapters.

[F1] - HELP	**[Shift]-[F1]** - PICK SELECTION
[F2] - VIEW DATA	**[Shift]-[F2]** - DESIGN
[F3] - PREVIOUS	**[Shift]-[F3]** - FIND PREVIOUS
[F4] - NEXT	**[Shift]-[F4]** - FIND NEXT
[F5] - ADD/MODIFY FIELD	**[Shift]-[F5]** - FIND
[F6] - EXTEND	**[Shift]-[F6]** - REPLACE
[F7] - MOVE	**[Shift]-[F7]** - SIZE
[F8] - COPY	**[Shift]-[F8]** - DITTO
[F9] - ZOOM	**[Shift]-[F9]** - QUICK REPORT
[F10] - MENU	**[Shift]-[F10]** - MACROS

At the Dot Prompt the function keys are programmed to execute the following commands:

[F1] - HELP	**[F6]** - DISPLAY STATUS
[F2] - ASSIST	**[F7]** - DISPLAY MEMORY
[F3] - LIST	**[F8]** - DISPLAY
[F4] - DIR	**[F9]** - APPEND
[F5] - DISPLAY STRUCTURE	**[F10]** - EDIT

Shift is not used with the function keys in Dot Prompt mode.

Exiting dBASE IV from the Control Center

To exit dBASE IV from the Control Center,

1. Press **[Alt]-[E]** to open the Exit menu.
2. Either type the letter **Q** or position the highlight bar on the **Quit to DOS** option (as shown in Figure I-5) and press **[Enter]**, and you will be returned to the DOS prompt.

NOTE: Wait until the DOS prompt appears before turning off the computer. This will ensure that the disk drives are not in use and that the database files and programs are closed.

Turn off the computer, remove your work disk from drive A, and store it safely. You will use it in later lessons.

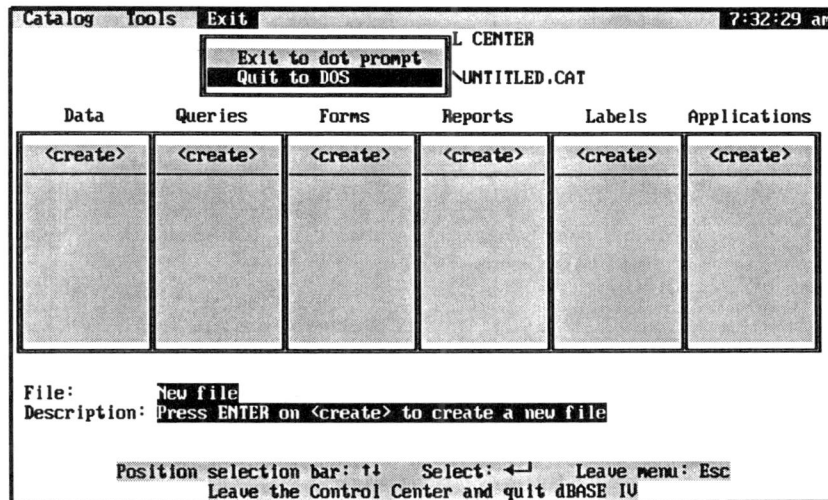

Figure I-5:
Exiting from the Control Center

Review Exercises

1. Follow the five steps described in the text to load your dBASE IV program.
2. Practice moving from the ASSIST mode to the Dot Prompt mode. Return to the ASSIST mode.
3. Open the Catalog menu and use the up and down arrow keys to highlight each available command in the menu. Notice how information on the navigation line and message line changes as you highlight new commands. Notice that the highlight bar jumps over the dim choices.
4. Open the Tools menu, and then close it.
5. Follow the steps described in the text to exit dBASE IV from the ASSIST mode.
6. Turn off your computer.

1

Creating a Database File

The objectives of this lesson are to
- Use the Help facility
- Create a database file
- Create a record field structure
- Add a description to a file
- Append records
- Display data in the file
- Close a database file
- Make a backup copy of your file
- Add a file to the current catalog

Defining the Components of a Database

A database is a computer file that holds information in the same way a telephone book does. Each person listed in the phone book has a name, an address (usually), and a phone number. In a database, the set of information about that phone customer would be called a record.

A record is one listing--in this case, one customer. The individual items of information about that customer are called fields. In the phone book, the fields are the customer's name, address, and phone number. A record is made up of fields of information; a database is made up of records.

In order to store information effectively, all records in a database contain the same fields. Thus, the phone book entries list the customer's name along with his or her phone number, because a phone number without an associated name is not a very useful piece of information. Addresses are not crucial in using the phone, but they may be helpful in locating the right person. The phone book therefore lists addresses, but they are optional. Because some customer records contain addresses, there is a field for addresses, although this field may not always be used.

Whether or not a field always contains information, it must exist in the record if you intend to store that particular type of information in the database at all. When you begin to build a database, you need to determine what types of information you want to store in the database and make sure you create a field for each item. As you build a database, you define a record structure; that is, you specify how many fields each record will contain and what kind of information you will enter into these fields. As you define the record structure, you can designate fields to be numeric fields, which allows you to perform arithmetic operations on them. For example, if you created a field for "current account balance," you could add the balances for all of the records and obtain the total amount owed—a very useful and time-saving step.

Creating a record structure that has a place for all of the information you want in your database is the first step in building a good database.

Using the Help Facility

Before you begin to build a database, you need to know how to obtain help if you get into trouble. Whenever you encounter difficulties, have a question, or want to learn more, the dBASE Help facility is ready to offer assistance. Help is available from a file within dBASE IV itself.

Help is "context sensitive." That means that whatever you are in the midst of doing, when you press the **[F1]** help key, dBASE will show you the closest help screen to your current operation. Once in the Help system, you can print the current help screen, call for the Table of Contents, get a list of Related Topics, or Backup to a previous screen.

To obtain help on whatever you are doing in ASSIST mode, keep the highlight on top of that command or menu item, and press the **[F1]** Help key.

1.   Place the highlight on top of <create> in the Data panel and Press **[F1]**.
       The "HELP: Create Database Files" screen appears (as shown in Figure 1-1).

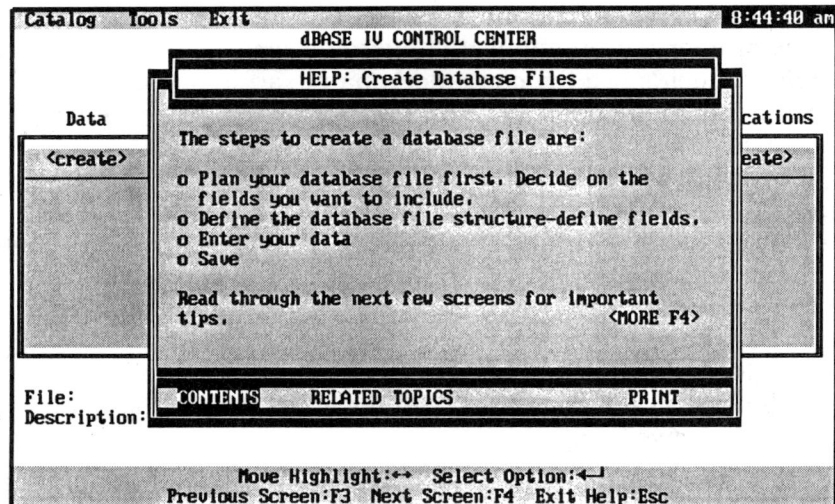

Figure 1-1: The Help Screen

Note the Navigation line's message that the [F4] key will move to the Next Screen and the [F3] key will show the previous screen of help.

2.   Press [F4].
     Note the new information and,
3.   Press [F4] a second time.

At the bottom of the help window are four "buttons." CONTENTS will display the Help system's Table of Contents. RELATED TOPICS will pop up a list of topics related to the current screen's information. BACKUP will move to the previous screen that you viewed. PRINT will copy the current help information to the printer. To select a button, press its first letter.

To print the current help screen showing Field Types,
1.   Press **P**.
2.   Press **B** to BACKUP to the Defining Fields help screen.
3.   Press **R** to display a list of RELATED TOPICS.
     To select a Related Topic, move up or down in the list with the down arrow [↓] or the up arrow [↑], and, when the highlight is on the desired topic, press [Enter].
4.   Move the highlight on top of MODIFY STRUCTURE (as shown in Figure 1-2).

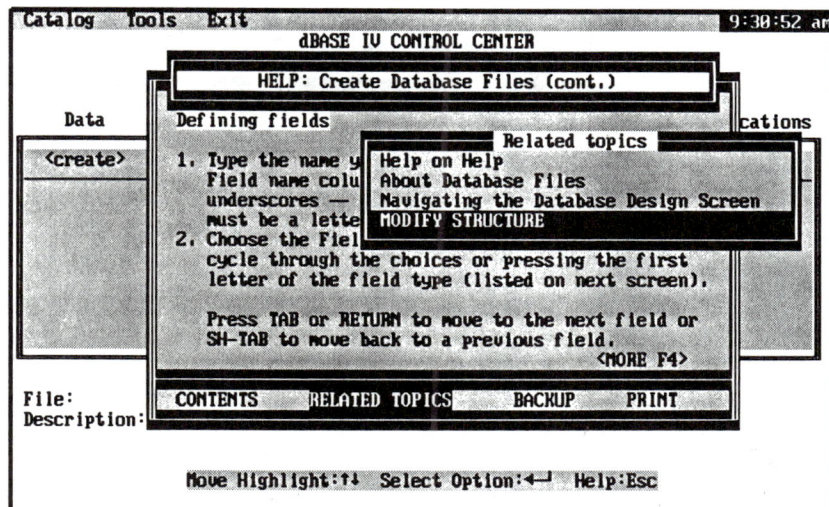

Figure 1-2: *Related Topics in Help Mode*

5.   Press [Enter].
     This screen explains modifying the structure of a database, an operation you will do in the next chapter.
6.   Press [Esc] to return to the ASSIST mode's Control Center.

Setting the Default Drive

In this tutorial, you will use your work disk in drive A. You therefore need to set the default drive to drive A. The default drive is the disk drive where dBASE IV expects to find your data files. You will need to set the default drive each time you enter dBASE IV.

To change the default drive and path now,

1. Press **[Alt]-[T]** to open the Tools menu.
2. Select **DOS utilities** by typing a **D** or by moving the highlight on top of it and pressing **[Enter]**.
   The "DOS util" screen will appear, containing its own menu bar with options for working with files on the disk drives.
   To change the default drive,
3. Open the DOS menu by pressing **[Alt]-[D]**.
4. Select **Set default drive:directory** by pressing **S** or by highlighting the choice and pressing **[Enter]**.
5. Type **A:** on top of whatever drive and directory shows, delete any remaining characters (as shown in Figure 1-3), and press **[Enter]**.

Figure 1-3:
Setting the Drive

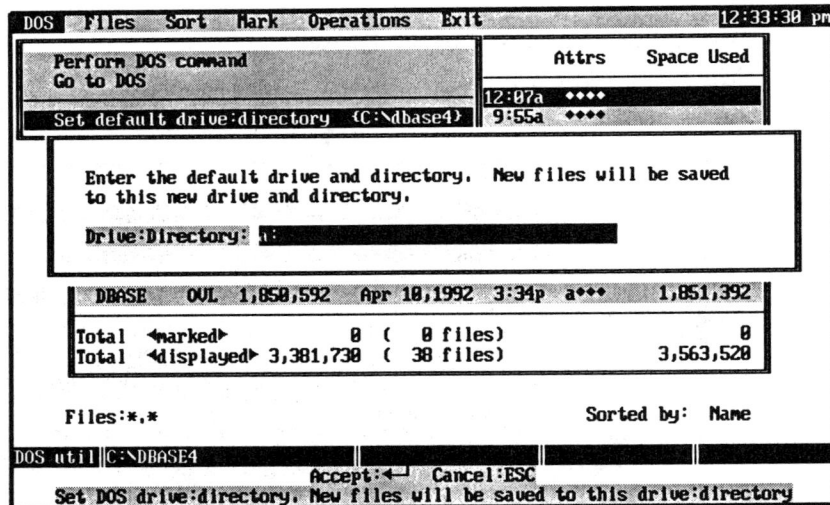

```
DOS   Files   Sort   Mark   Operations   Exit                12:33:30 pm
┌─────────────────────────────────┬──────────────────────────┐
│ Perform DOS command             │   Attrs    Space Used    │
│ Go to DOS                       ├──────────────────────────┤
│                                 │ 12:07a  ◆◆◆◆             │
│ Set default drive:directory  <C:\dbase4> │ 9:55a  ◆◆◆◆        │
├─────────────────────────────────────────────────────────────┤
│                                                              │
│  Enter the default drive and directory.  New files will be saved │
│  to this new drive and directory.                            │
│                                                              │
│  Drive:Directory: A:                                         │
│                                                              │
├──────────────────────────────────────────────────────────────┤
│  DBASE    OVL  1,050,592   Apr 10,1992  3:34p  a◆◆◆  1,051,392 │
├──────────────────────────────────────────────────────────────┤
│ Total ◄marked►            0  (   0 files)                  0 │
│ Total ◄displayed► 3,381,730  (  38 files)          3,563,520 │
│                                                              │
│  Files:*.*                              Sorted by:  Name     │
├──────────────────────────────────────────────────────────────┤
│ DOS util│C:\DBASE4                                           │
│                      Accept:◄┘  Cancel:ESC                   │
│  Set DOS drive:directory. New files will be saved to this drive:directory │
└──────────────────────────────────────────────────────────────┘
```

The display on the DOS util screen will not change when you change the default drive. The displayed files are controlled by Change drive:directory in the Files menu. This useful distinction exists to allow you to view and operate on files in a directory other than the current default.

You have switched the default drive to A:. To exit back to the Control Center,

6. Press **[Alt]-[E]** to open the Exit menu.
7. Select **Exit to Control Center** by pressing either **E** or the **[Enter]** key.

The fourth line down on the Control Center screen should now show the catalog as A:\UNTITLED.CAT. If it does not say A:, perform steps 1 through 7 again. If the catalog name is not UNTITLED.CAT (or if file names appear in the task panels), your data disk has been used previously. You should obtain a fresh diskette and repeat steps 1-7.

Creating a Database File

When you build a database or create a database in dBASE IV, you will begin with these three steps:

1. Determining a record structure;
2. Naming the file;
3. Entering data.

To create a database file named MASTER,

1. Highlight <create> in the Data panel and press **[Enter]**.

Before you begin to create your database file, turn the **[CapsLock]** key on. You will see the word "Caps" on the status bar in the lower right area of the screen. When you type, the letters will all appear in uppercase.

dBASE IV presents the database design screen that requests information about the first field in the database, as shown in Figure 1-4. You will assign a name to this field and describe the format of the data to be stored in it.

Figure 1-4:
Setting Up
Field
Parameters

Num	Field Name	Field Type	Width	Dec	Index
1		Character			Y

Bytes remaining: 4000

Database A:\<NEW>   Field 1/1   Caps
Enter the field name. Insert/Delete field:Ctrl-N/Ctrl-U
Field names begin with a letter and may contain letters, digits and underscores

To create the record structure for the MASTER database, you will enter the information contained in Table 1-1. Before you type in the information contained in Table 1-1, read the following explanations so that you understand what each of the components represents:

1. **FIELD NAME.** The field name should represent the field's contents. For example, a field that contains customers' ZIP codes might be named ZIP or ZIPCODE. A field name can contain up to 10 characters. It must start with a letter and can contain additional letters, digits, and the underscore; however, it cannot contain spaces.

2. **FIELD TYPE**. The field type indicates whether the field's contents are character/alphabetic (C), numeric with a fixed number of decimal places (N), floating point numeric (F), a date (D), logical (L), or memo (M). The default field type is character, and the word "character" automatically appears in the highlighted space for field type. You can change the field type by pressing the first letter of the type you want or by pressing the space bar until the correct type appears and then pressing **[Enter]**.

3. **FIELD WIDTH**. You will specify in numeric terms the number of spaces that you want to set aside for the field contents. A character field can contain from 1 to 254 characters; a numeric or floating point field can contain from 1 to 20 digits, including a positive/negative sign and decimal point; a date automatically contains 8 digits (YYYYMMDD); a logical field automatically takes a width of 1; and a memo field may contain a varying number of characters.

4. **DEC**. DEC allows you to specify the number of decimal places (0-18) that you want in a numeric or floating point field. (When you define a non-numeric field, the cursor automatically skips DEC and goes to the next field.) The number of decimal places must be at least 2 places less than the number specified for the numeric field's width to allow for the decimal point and sign.

5. **INDEX**. A Y in this column directs dBASE IV to automatically create an index based on this single field. An index is one way to keep the data in alphabetical or numerical order. We will explore indexes in a later chapter.

   After you have entered the field name, type, width, decimal places, and index for the first field, the system will request the same information for subsequent fields, until you tell the system that there are no further fields to define. At this point, the record structure for the database is complete.

Table 1-1 shows the record structure of the MASTER file's eight fields.

Field Number	Field Name	Field Type	Width	Dec	Index
1	ACCT_NUM	N	6	0	N
2	CUST_NAME	C	20		N
3	STREET	C	20		N
4	CITY_STATE	C	15		N
5	ZIP	C	9		N
6	BEGIN_BAL	N	10	2	N
7	UPDATE_BAL	N	10	2	N
8	CR_LIMIT	N	10	2	N

Table 1-1: *The MASTER File Fields*

To enter the field name and specifications for the first field,

1. Type **ACCT_NUM** in the blank below the heading Field Name and press **[Enter]**.
2. Press **N** to change the field type from character to numeric.
3. Type **6** and press **[Enter]** to enter the field width.
4. Type **0** and press **[Enter]** to enter the number of decimal places.
5. Press **[Enter]** to confirm the N in the Index column and move to line 2.
    You have now defined the first field in the MASTER file. To define the second field, CUST_NAME,
6. Type **CUST_NAME** under the Field Name heading and press **[Enter]**.
    Leaving character as the setting for field type,
7. Press the right arrow **[→]** cursor key or **[Enter]** to go to the Width column.
8. Type **20** and press **[Enter]**.
9. Press **[Enter]** to confirm the N in the Index column.
    You are now ready to define field 3. Starting with STREET and ending with field 8,
10. Enter the remaining lines from Table 1-1. (The finished record structure is shown in Figure 1-5.)
    After creating the final field (CR_LIMIT),
11. Press **[Alt]-[E]** to open the Exit menu and type an **S** to select **Save changes and exit**.
    When the prompt asks you to
    Save as:

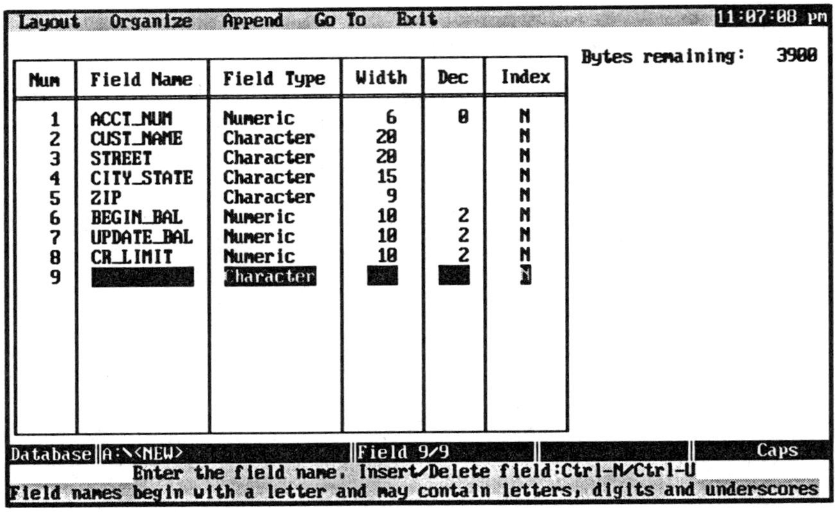

Figure 1-5:
Table 1-1
Record
Structure

12. Type **MASTER** (as shown in Figure 1-6) and press **[Enter]** and
    you will be returned to the Control Center. (If dBASE IV asks
    Input data records now? [Y/N]
    Press **N**.)

*Note: File names can contain from 1 to 8 letters and digits. dBASE IV automatically
adds the three-character file extension .DBF to indicate that the file is a DataBase
File.*

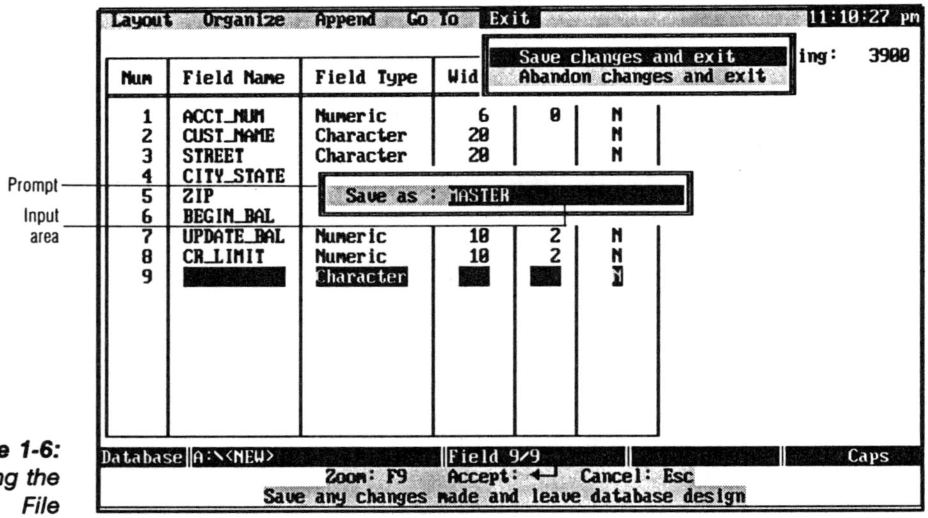

Figure 1-6:
Naming the
File

You have now created a file called MASTER, defined the number of
fields that will exist in each record, and defined the field names, types
of fields, and the lengths of the fields. The Control Center shows the
MASTER table above the horizontal line in the Data panel (as shown in
Figure 1-7), meaning that the file is immediately open and available for
use.

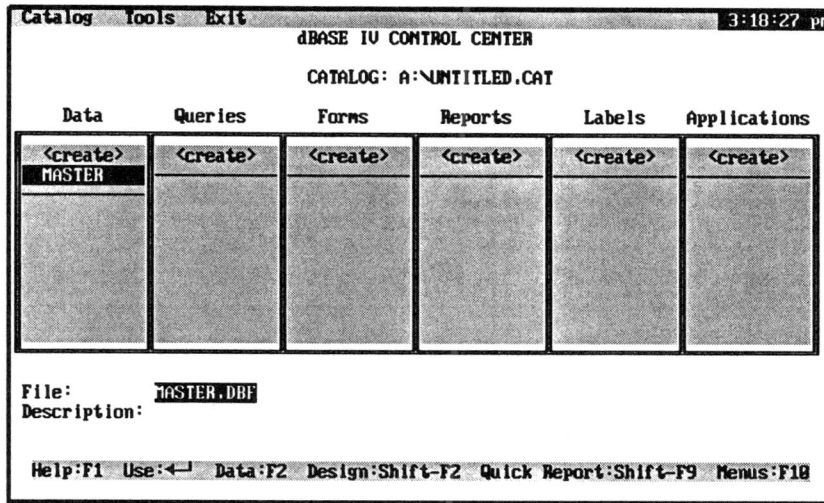

Figure 1-7:
The Open
File

Adding a Description to the File

To add a file description,

1. If necessary, move the highlight on top of the name MASTER in the Data panel.
2. Press **[Alt]-[C]** to open the Catalog menu.
3. Press **C** to select **Change description of highlighted file**.
4. Type the description **MASTER FILE OF CUSTOMER BALANCES** and press **[Enter]** (as shown in Figure 1-8).

Look below the task panels at the File name and Description lines to see the new description.

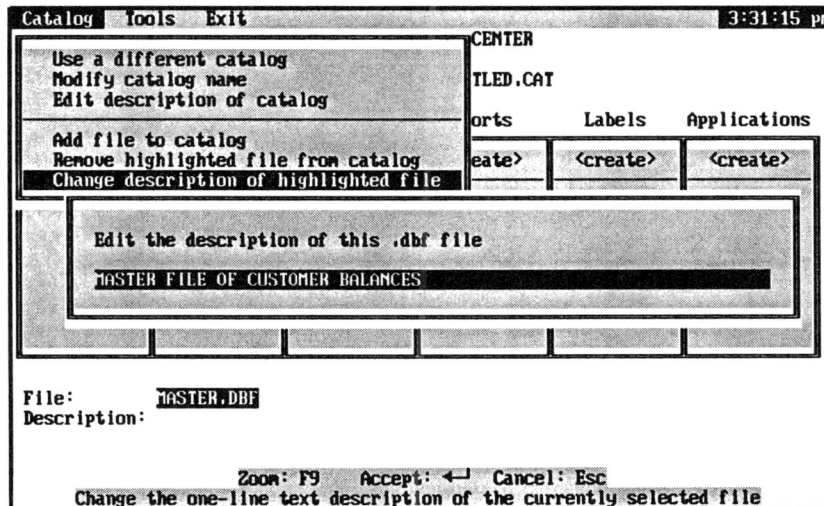

Figure 1-8:
Editing the
File's
Description

Adding Data to the Database with Append

There are several ways to add data to a database in dBASE IV. The Append command is perhaps the most direct. When you use this command, you are in essence telling dBASE IV that you want to add more records to the end of the database, even though the database really contains no records at this point.

To use the Append command to enter data,

1. Be certain that the highlight in on top of MASTER and press **[Enter]**.
    A dialog box containing three possible actions to take with the MASTER database file will appear (as shown in Figure 1-9).

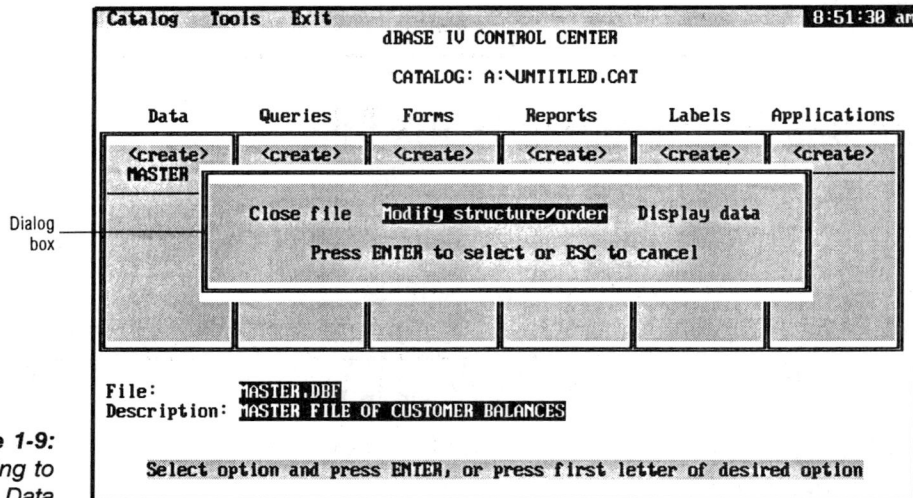

Figure 1-9: Preparing to Append Data

To select **Modify structure/order**,
2. Type an **M** or move the highlight onto **Modify structure/order** and press **[Enter]**.
    On the Database screen,
3. Open the Append menu with **[Alt]-[A]** or by pressing the right arrow **[→]** (as shown in Figure 1-10).
4. Select **Enter records from keyboard** by pressing **E** or highlighting that choice and pressing **[Enter]**.

The Edit screen (as shown in Figure 1-11) will appear. You can now begin to enter data into your database. Start by entering information in the first field of the first record, and then filling in the rest of the information for that record. After you have entered all of the information for the first record, go on to the next record and continue entering data until you have entered the five records shown in Table 1-2. If you should make an error while entering data into a field, correct the error by using the **[BackSpace]** key to delete the character(s) you have mistakenly typed. If you notice the error only after pressing **[Enter]** to move to another field, you can use the cursor movement keys to return to the field in which the error occurs and then strike the **[BackSpace]** key to correct the error.

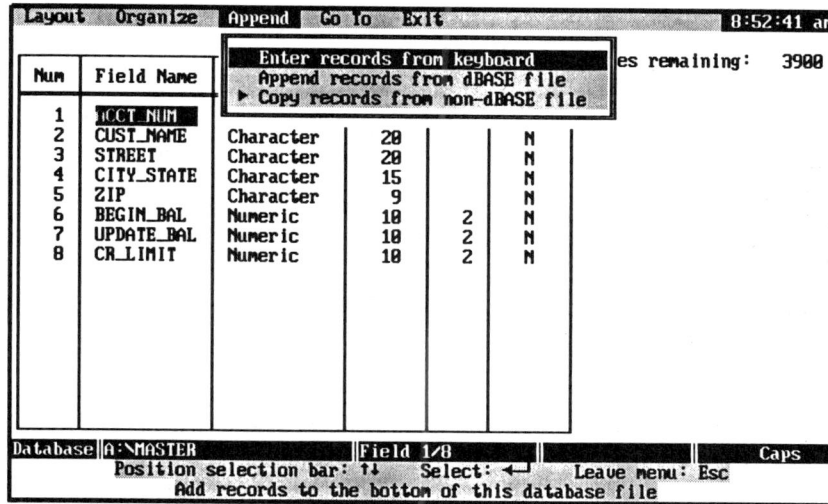

Figure 1-10:
The Append Menu

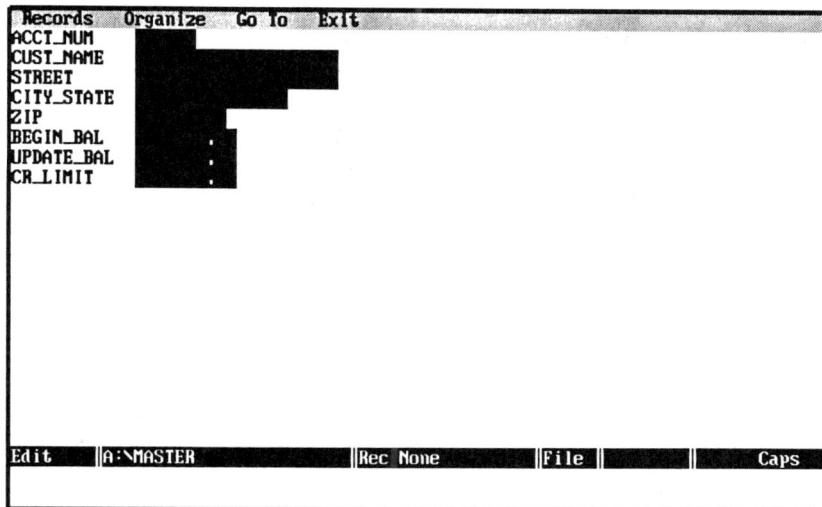

Figure 1-11:
Screen for Appending Data

With the cursor in the ACCT_NUM field,

1. Type **2145** and press **[Enter]**.
   When the cursor moves to the next field, where you will enter the customer name MURPHY,
2. Type **MURPHY** and press **[Enter]**.
   The cursor will then move on to the third field.
3. Finish entering data for the first record according to Table 1-2. Be sure to type the decimal point when needed.

Field Name	Record 1	Record 2	Record 3	Record 4	Record 5
ACCT_NUM	2145	4115	4155	6598	6155
CUST_NAME	MURPHY	ADAMS	JONES	MCCLURE	ODEGARD
STREET	23 OAK	412 ELM	345 ELM	986 OAK	98 ELM
CITY_STATE	LEE, IL	MAR, CA	LEE, IL	LEE, IL	OAK, CA
ZIP	78374	95485	78374	78374	96254
BEGIN_BAL	150.00	200.00	300.00	300.00	100.00
UPDATE_BAL	150.00	600.00	300.00	500.00	400.00
CR_LIMIT	4000.00	3000.00	2000.00	1000.00	2500.00

Table 1-2: *The MASTER File Records*

If the data item completely fills the field width, as it would for a customer name that contained 20 characters, the computer will beep and the cursor will automatically move to the next field. (The computer will also beep if you should mistakenly try to enter the wrong type of data in a field; for example, if you attempted to enter alphabetic data in a field specified as numeric.)

When you press **[Enter]** after you have finished entering data into a numeric field, the characters in that field are automatically right-justified. Pressing the decimal point (.) in a numeric field also right-justifies the entry even before you press **[Enter]**.

When you have entered data for the last field in a record, a new, blank record will appear on the screen so that you can begin to enter data in the next record.

NOTE: When you enter decimal numbers, enter the numbers from left to right, pressing the period (.) key to enter the decimal point. If the numbers to the right of the decimal are zeros, you do not need to enter them: dBASE IV will enter them automatically.

The dBASE IV system will align decimal numbers according to the number of decimal places defined in the file structure. For example, if the number you want to enter is 5.00 and you simply type 5 and press [Enter], the system will record the number as 5.00.

4. Enter the remaining data given in Table 1-2 for records 2 through 5.

When you reach the last record, for the customer named Odegard (as shown in Figure 1-12), **do not** press **[Enter]** after you type the amount $2500.00 in the CR_LIMIT field. (If you do press **[Enter]**, press **PgUp** to come back to record 5.) Instead, to save the records and return to the Control Center,

5. Press **[Alt]-[E]** to open the Exit menu.

6. Select **Exit** and the Database screen reappears.
    To return to the Control Center,
7. Press **[Alt]-[E]** to open the Exit menu.
8. Select **Save changes and exit**.
    When dBASE IV says at the bottom of the screen **Press ENTER key to confirm...**,
9. Press **[Enter]**.

Highlighted data entry area corresponds to field size

Figure 1-12:
The Final
MASTER
Record

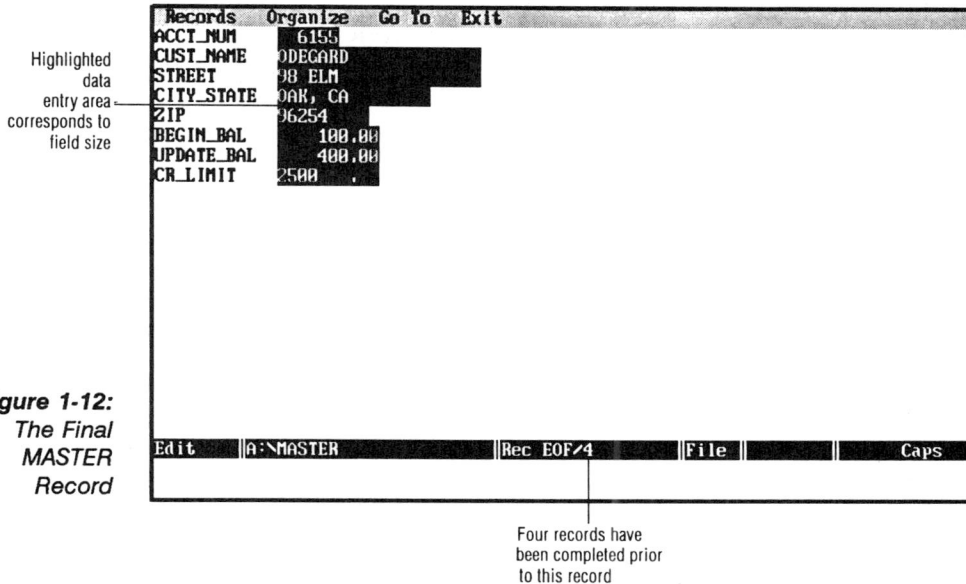

Four records have been completed prior to this record

You have saved the records and returned to the Control Center. MASTER is still above the horizontal line in the Data panel because it is still the open database file.

Viewing the Data Entries in Edit mode

To display your database entries on the screen,

1. Be certain the highlight bar is on top of MASTER, and press **[Enter]**.
2. Either press **D**, or highlight **Display data** and press **[Enter]**.
    The Edit screen will reappear with one of the records showing. Examine the third section of the status bar to determine which record of the five you are looking at.
3. Press **[PgDn]** one or more times to move to the next record.
4. Press **[PgUp]** to move to the previous record.
    To move to the ZIP field,
5. Press the down arrow **[↓]** four times.
    To return to the ACCT_NUM field,
6. Press the up arrow **[↑]** four times.
    To move to the first record,
7. Press **[Ctrl]-[PgUp]**.

NOTE: Should you try to move to a record ahead of number 1, nothing will happen; if you try to move past the last record, dBASE IV will ask at the bottom of the screen "Add new records? (Y/N)." Press N to answer No and you will remain on the last record, record 5.

Viewing the Data Entries in Browse Mode

A different arrangement for displaying the data on the screen is called Browse mode. Edit mode and Browse mode show exactly the same data, but organize it differently on the screen. Edit mode shows one record at a time, but many fields. Browse mode displays many records at a time, but only as many fields as will fit on the width of the screen. Each mode has advantages and times when it is preferable.

To switch from the current Edit mode to Browse mode,

1.   Press **[F2]**.
      To switch back to Edit mode,
2.   Press **[F2]** again.
      To return to Browse mode once more,
3.   Press **[F2]**.

Moving about in a database table in Browse mode is done mostly with the **[Tab]** key to move to the right one field at a time, or **[Shift]-[Tab]** to move to the left. The screen will scroll sideways when the cursor gets to the edge of the screen. The arrow keys move one character sideways or one line vertically at a time. **[PgDn]** and **[PgUp]** move a screenful of listings downward or upward.

To move to the last field (CR_LIMIT) of record one,

1.   Press **[Tab]** seven times.
2.   Press **[Tab]** one more time and note that the cursor wraps around to the first field, but has dropped to record two.
3.   Press **[Shift]-[Tab]** to wrap back to the end of record one.
4.   Press **[Home]** to return to the first field (ACCT_NUM).
      To return to the Control Center,
5.   Press **[Alt]-[E]** to open the Exit menu.
6.   Select **Exit**.

MASTER is still above the horizontal line in the Data panel, so it is still open.

Closing a Database File

When you close a database file, any final changes to the data will be recorded, and the filename will move below the horizontal line in the Data panel.

To close the open database file,

1.   Be certain the highlight is on top of the filename and press **[Enter]**.

2. Select **Close file** in the resulting dialog box by pressing either **C** or **[Enter]**.

Creating a Second Database File

As a practice exercise, you will create a transaction file for accounts receivable. Again, you need to design the structure first. Table 1-3 shows the structure for ARTRAN, the accounts receivable transaction file. ARTRAN contains seven fields. Note that the sixth field is a date field. By default, date fields are eight characters with a format of month/day/year.

1. Move the highlight bar on top of <create> in the Data panel and press **[Enter]**.
    The utility screen for defining the record structure appears. You used this utility earlier to enter the record structure for the MASTER file. This time, you will enter the structure for ARTR-AN. Using the information from Table 1-3, enter the information for the seven fields.
    When you have finished entering the seventh field,
2. Press **[Alt]-[E]**.
3. Type **S** to select **Save changes and exit**.
4. Type the name **ARTRAN** in the **Save as:** box and press **[Enter]**.
    You are returned to the Control Center.

Field Number	Field Name	Field Type	Width	Dec	Index
1	ACCT_NUM	N	6	0	N
2	REF_NO	N	6	0	N
3	TRAN_CD	N	1	0	N
4	PROD_CD	N	2	0	N
5	AGE_CD	N	1	0	N
6	DATE	D	8		N
7	AMOUNT	N	10	2	N

Table 1-3: *The ARTRAN File Fields*

You will now enter the data for each field. A quicker way to get to the Edit screen for data entry is to place the highlight on top of the file-name in the Data panel, press **[Enter]**, and select "Display data." This moves directly to the Edit screen.

5. With the highlight on top of ARTRAN, press **[Enter]**.
6. Press **D** to select Display data.

7.   Enter data for the four records from Table 1-4.

When you enter the $10.00 in the AMOUNT field for record 4, you will automatically be given a form for record 5. **Do not** save and exit on an empty record, or the undesirable empty record will be saved.

Field Name	Record 1	Record 2	Record 3	Record 4
ACCT_NUM	6598	6155	2145	4155
REF_NO	11458	11459	77145	77146
TRAN_CD	4	4	1	1
PROD_CD	0	0	45	39
AGE_CD	1	1	0	0
DATE	011788	011788	011788	011788
AMOUNT	-75.00	-13.50	50.00	10.00

Table 1-4: *The ARTRAN File Records*

To get back to the filled in record 4,

8.   Press **[PgUp]**.
9.   Press **[Alt]-[E]** to open the Exit menu.
10.   Select **Exit**, and you will be returned to the Control Center.
To display the data you entered,
11.   With the highlight on top of ARTRAN press **[Enter]**.
12.   In the dialog box press **D** to select **Display data**.
13.   Press **[F2]** to switch to Browse mode.
Notice in the Status Bar that you are on the last record (Rec 4/4), so that only the last record is showing. To display the rest of the records (as shown in Figure 1-13),
14.   Press **[PgUp]**.

If you notice any errors, do not try to correct them now. You will learn how to edit data later.

15.   Press **[Alt]-[E]** to open the Exit menu and pick **Exit** to return to the Control Center.

Making a Backup Copy of Your Database

In business, the accounts receivable master file is very important: it indicates how much money customers owe the company. If it were to become lost or damaged, the company could suffer serious consequences. Therefore, many businesses insist on making backup copies of crucial computer files. In dBASE IV, you can copy a disk file in the DOS utilities.

In the following procedure, you will copy the file ARTRAN to a backup file, ARTRANBU (in which BU stands for Back Up), on the same disk.

ACCT_NUM	REF_NO	TRAN_CD	PROD_CD	AGE_CD	DATE	AMOUNT
6598	11458	4	0	1	09/17/92	-75.00
6155	11459	4	0	1	09/17/92	-13.50
2145	77145	1	45	0	09/17/92	50.00
4155	77146	1	39	0	09/18/92	10.00

Records Organize Fields Go To Exit

Browse A:\ARTRAN Rec 1/4 File Caps

Figure 1-13:
Listing the
ARTRAN
Records

To copy a database file to a file of another name,

1. Type **[Alt]-[T]** to open the Tools menu.
2. Select **DOS utilities** by pressing **D**.
   On the DOS util screen,
3. Move the highlight on top of **ARTRAN** and press the **[Alt]** key together with the letter **O** (**[Alt]-[O]**) to open the Operations menu (as shown in Figure 1-14).
4. Press **C** to select **Copy**.
5. Type **S** to choose **Single File** since it's only the one file that we wish to copy.
   In the resulting dialog box (see Figure 1-15) the filename to be copied is under the word **Copy**.
   Also, the Drive:Directory is correctly filled in as A:.
   We need to fill in the Filename, so,
6. Press **[Enter]** to move over to the Filename section, and
7. Type **ARTRANBU.DBF**.
8. Press **[Ctrl]-[End]** as prompted in the navigation line at the bottom of the screen to perform the copy.
   The screen display will be redrawn and ARTRANBU should be listed.
9. Press **[Alt]-[E]** to open the Exit menu and select **Exit to Control Center**.

```
 DOS   Files   Sort   Mark   Operations   Exit                      11:16:56 am

     Name/Extension        S │ ▶ Delete │ Time       Attrs    Space Used
                             │ ▶ Copy   │
     ARTRAN    DBF           │ ▶ Move   │ 1992 10:14a  a◆◆◆         1,024
     CATALOG   CAT           │ ▶ Rename │ 1992 11:10a  a◆◆◆         1,024
     MASTER    DBF           │   View   │ 1992 10:41a  a◆◆◆         1,024
     UNTITLED  CAT           │   Edit   │ 1992 11:12a  a◆◆◆         1,024

    Total  ◀marked▶              0  (    0 files)                        0
    Total  ◀displayed▶       2,112  (    4 files)                    4,096

    Files:*.*                                         Sorted by:  Name



 DOS util A:\
              Position selection bar:↑↓  Select:◄┘   Leave menu:ESC
                     Copy file(s) to another directory
```

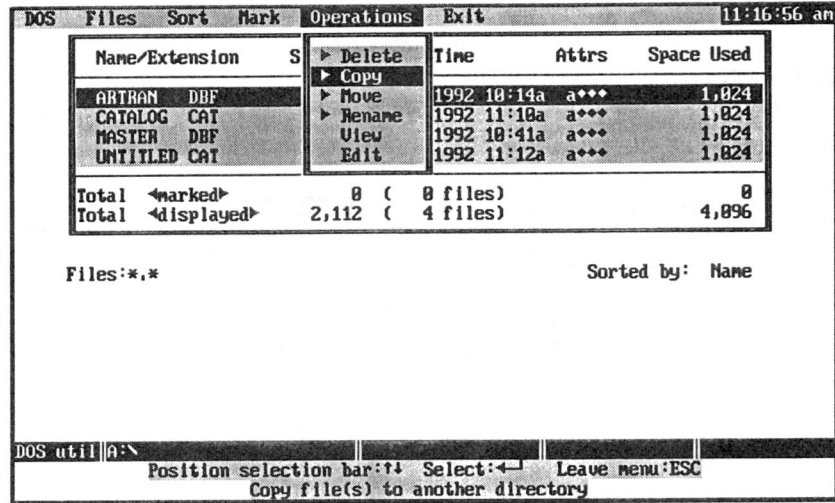

Figure 1-14:
The Operations Menu

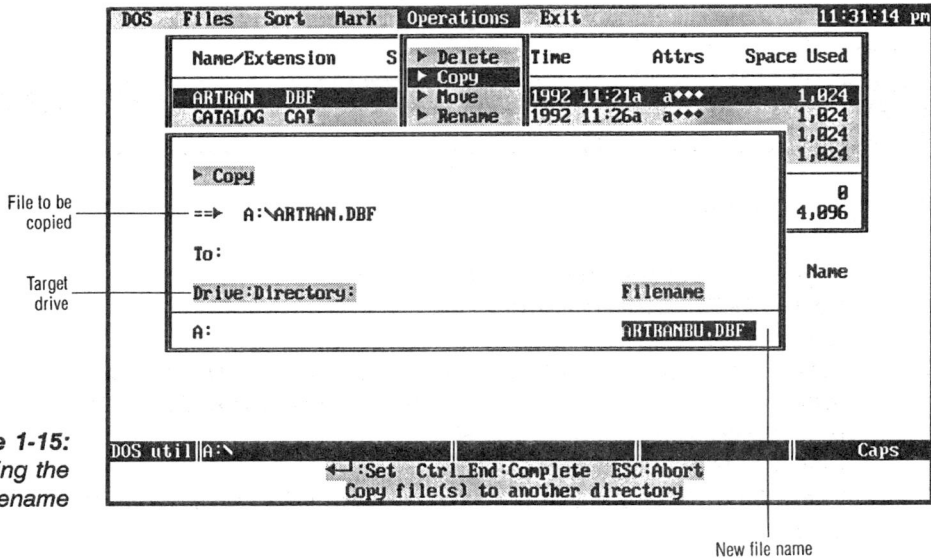

```
 DOS   Files   Sort   Mark   Operations   Exit                      11:31:14 pm

     Name/Extension        S │ ▶ Delete │ Time       Attrs    Space Used
                             │ ▶ Copy   │
     ARTRAN    DBF           │ ▶ Move   │ 1992 11:21a  a◆◆◆         1,024
     CATALOG   CAT           │ ▶ Rename │ 1992 11:26a  a◆◆◆         1,024
                                                                    1,024
                                                                    1,024
   ┌──────────────────────────────────────────────────┐
   │ ▶ Copy                                            │                  0
   │                                                   │              4,096
   │ ==▶   A:\ARTRAN.DBF                               │
   │                                                   │
   │ To:                                               │            Name
   │                                                   │
   │ Drive:Directory:                   Filename       │
   │                                                   │
   │ A:                                 ARTRANBU.DBF   │
   └──────────────────────────────────────────────────┘

 DOS util A:\                                                       Caps
              ◄┘:Set   Ctrl_End:Complete   ESC:Abort
                     Copy file(s) to another directory
```

File to be
copied

Target
drive

Figure 1-15:
*Entering the
Filename*

New file name

   You have now created a backup copy of ARTRAN, which will be
helpful in case any damage should occur to the ARTRAN file. This copy
will also be useful when you modify your original database in later
lessons: You will still be able to refer to a copy of your original database. From time to time in the tutorial, you will use the backup copy of
the database.
   It is a good idea to back up your database files regularly. If the file
contains important data, such as information about accounts receivable, you should make more than one copy and store at least one copy
on a different disk in a different location from your computer and
original data. This will ensure the safety of your database files and
prevent the loss of valuable time and data.

Adding a File to the Catalog

The ARTRANBU file that we just copied does not show up in the Data panel. Any file directly created on dBASE IV's design screens (like MASTER or ARTRAN) is automatically added to the current catalog, but copied files are not. To add ARTRANBU to the catalog (and thus the Data panel), we must use the Catalog menu. To add the proper type of file, the highlight bar **must** be in the task panel of the correct type. Since we want to add a database file, the highlight must be in the Data panel.

1.   Move the highlight into the Data panel.
2.   Press **[Alt]-[C]** to open the Catalog menu.
3.   Select **Add file to catalog** by pressing **A**.
     A list of the available database files on the active disk will appear (see Figure 1-16).

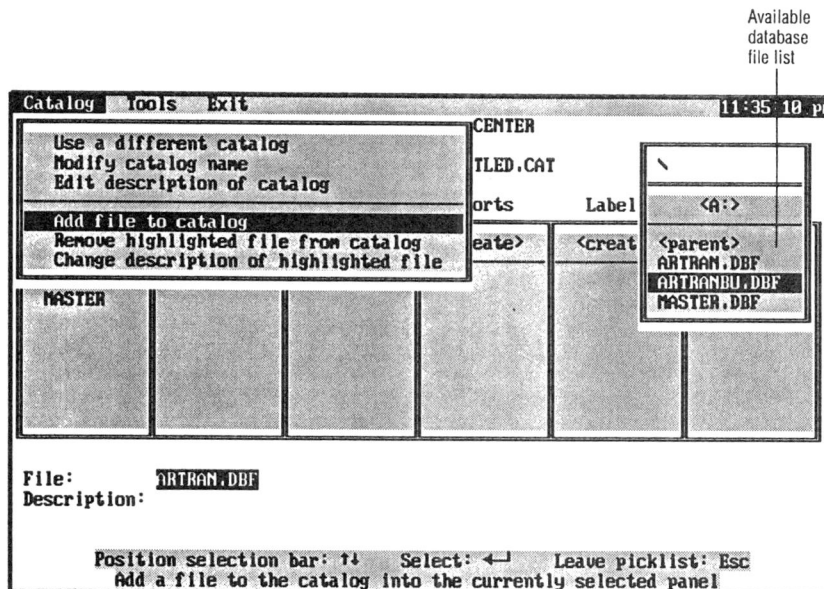

Figure 1-16:
Adding a File
to the
Catalog

4.   Move the highlight bar on top of **ARTRANBU.DBF** and press **[Enter]**.
     A box for editing the description of the file appears. To specify the description,
5.   Type **BACKUP OF ARTRAN FILE** and press **[Enter]**.
     To verify the file and description,
6.   Move the highlight bar on top of ARTRANBU and examine the File and Description lines.

Finally, we will close all files. This not only keeps the display tidy, but records any last changes to the file. Properly quitting will also close any open file.

To close ARTRAN, move the highlight bar on top of ARTRAN and

1. Press **[Enter]**.
2. Select **Close file** by typing **C**.
    There is now no active database in memory.

Review Exercises

1. While in the Control Center put the highlight on "Add file to catalog" in the Catalog menu. Use the Help facility to reference help on this topic; then exit to the Control Center.
2. With the highlight on top of <create> in the Data panel, call the help system. Pick CONTENTS to access the Table of Contents and view the help screen referencing "Sort Data." Print this screen; then exit to the Control Center.
3. Set the default drive and path so that dBASE IV will look for your data files on drive A.
4. List the steps to create a database file in the ASSIST mode.
5. In the Control Center,
    A. Create a database file that contains fields for a person's name, street address, city, state, and zip code for each record. Name the file PRAC1.
    B. Enter five records into the file.
    C. Display the five records that you entered into the file in Edit mode, and also Browse mode.
    D. Close the file.

2

Editing and Searching a Database

The objectives of this lesson are to
- ▶ Retrieve a file
- ▶ Add a new field to an existing record structure
- ▶ Modify a field in an existing record structure
- ▶ Print a record field structure
- ▶ Go to a specific record
- ▶ Edit the contents of a record
- ▶ Display all records in Edit mode and Browse mode
- ▶ Append new records to an old file
- ▶ Mark and delete a record or records in a file
- ▶ Delete an existing file

Retrieving a File into Use in the ASSIST Mode

When you close a database file or exit properly from dBASE IV, the program automatically stores the file from memory to disk. At the end of Lesson 1, you closed the open file and may or may not have exited from dBASE IV. However, before you can use a database, it must be in memory. The process of bringing a file into memory is called "opening" a file, or retrieving or using a file. Taking a file out of memory is called "closing" a file. Before you can edit or modify a database, it must be open. To see if a database is open, look at the Data panel in the Control Center to see whether the filename is above the horizontal line, or look in the middle of the status bar on other screens. If the status bar shows a name of a database file, that file is in use. When you bring one database into use, the program automatically closes any other database that you may have been using before.

To bring a database into use in the Control Center when the database file is not currently in memory,

1. Move the highlight bar on top of the filename **MASTER** (as shown in Figure 2-1) and press **[Enter]**.
    In the resulting dialog box,
2. Either press **U** to select **Use file**, or with the highlight on top of **Use file** press **[Enter]**.

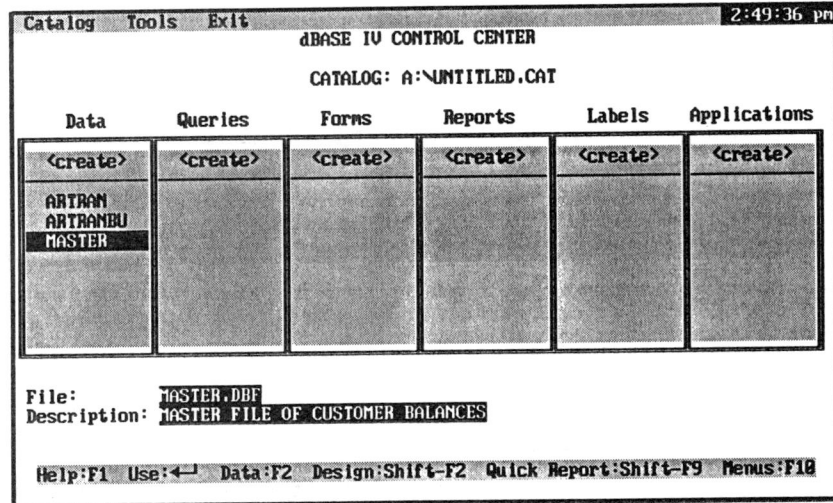

Figure 2-1:
Selecting the MASTER File

The filename moves above the horizontal bar in the Data panel and is now open and available for use.

Modifying the Structure of a Database

As you work with a database, you may find that the initial record structure you created is unsatisfactory: a field may not be big enough, or you may need to add a new field of information. Using the Database design screen, you can adjust the fields of the record structure. You may ask, why not just create a new database? The answer is that modifying an old file, whether or not it contains considerable data, is easier than creating a new one.

In the next two exercises, you will change the record structure, a process also called "modifying a database."

Adding a Field to the Record Structure

You will now modify the record structure of the MASTER file to include a memo field. A memo field is a field that can hold from 0 to 64,000 characters. dBASE IV automatically makes the field length 10 characters in the database file and stores the up to 64,000 characters of information in a separate file on the disk. That file will have the same basic name as the database file, but with the extension **.DBT**, instead of the database's **.DBF**. Whenever you open the database file, dBASE IV will handle the .DBT file automatically.

To add a memo field,

1. Place the highlight bar on top of MASTER and press **[Enter]**.
2. Type **M** to select **Modify structure/order**.

   Since you modify the order more often than the structure of a database, the Organize menu is automatically opened. To close the menu,
3. Press **[Esc]**.
4. Move the cursor to line **9** with the down arrow **[↓]**.
5. Type **TEXT** to name the new field and press **[Enter]**.
6. Press **M** to make TEXT a memo field.

   The remaining three columns are filled in automatically.
7. Press **[Alt]-[E]** to open the **Exit** menu.
8. Type **S** to select **Save changes and exit**.
9. Press **Y** to confirm the modification when asked "You have made changes. Are you sure you want to save these changes?"

   You will be returned to the Control Center.

Modifying Field Length in the Record Structure

In this exercise, you will change the width of the ZIP field to 10 characters.

With the highlight bar on top of MASTER,

1. Press **[Enter]**.
2. Type **M** for Modify structure/order.
3. Press **[Esc]** to close the Organize menu.
4. Position the cursor on the **ZIP** field **Width** column, type **10** (as shown in Figure 2-2), and press **[Enter]**.

Layout	Organize	Append	Go To	Exit			11:40:55 pm

Num	Field Name	Field Type	Width	Dec	Index
1	ACCT_NUM	Numeric	6	0	N
2	CUST_NAME	Character	20		N
3	STREET	Character	20		N
4	CITY_STATE	Character	15		N
5	ZIP	Character	10		N
6	BEGIN_BAL	Numeric	10	2	N
7	UPDATE_BAL	Numeric	10	2	N
8	CR_LIMIT	Numeric	10	2	N
9	TEXT	Memo	10		N

Bytes remaining: 3890

Database A:\MASTER   Field 5/9   Caps

Enter the field width
Character fields are 1 to 254 positions wide

Figure 2-2:
*Modifying
the ZIP Field
Width*

5. Press **[Alt]-[E]** to open the Exit menu.
6. Type **S** to select **Save changes and exit**.

7. Press **Y** to confirm the modification when asked "You have made changes. Are you sure you want to save these changes?"
    You will be returned to the Control Center.

Before the program returned to the Control Center, it changed all records in the database to the new record structure.

NOTE: If you change a field NAME when you modify a record structure, data in that field will not be copied to the modified field.
If you change the field type from character to numeric, any data in the field that is not numeric (that is, numbers) will be lost.
If you decrease the field size, the data in that field will be truncated to fit the new field size. Thus, data in the original field that extends beyond the new size will be lost.

Printing the Record Field Structure

To print the new record structure, with the highlight on MASTER,

1. Press **[Enter]**.
2. Type **M** for Modify structure/order.
3. Press **[Esc]** to close the Organize menu.
4. Press **[Alt]-[L]** to open the Layout menu.
5. Type **P** to select **Print database structure**.
6. Press **B** to **Begin printing**.

The record structure will be printed along with information about which file it represents, the number of records in the database, and the date of the last change to any part of the file, as shown in Figure 2-3.

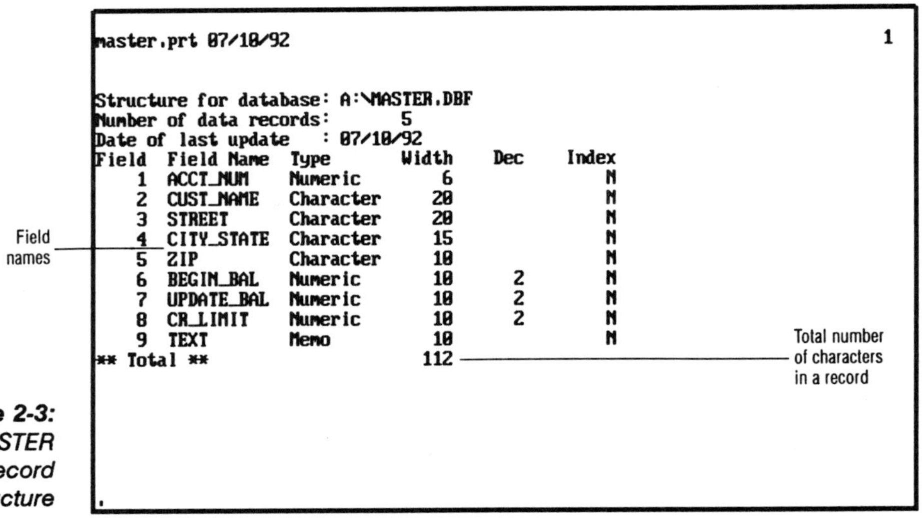

```
master.prt 07/10/92                                                    1


Structure for database: A:\MASTER.DBF
Number of data records:       5
Date of last update   : 07/10/92
Field  Field Name  Type       Width   Dec   Index
    1  ACCT_NUM    Numeric       6            N
    2  CUST_NAME   Character    20            N
    3  STREET      Character    20            N
    4  CITY_STATE  Character    15            N
    5  ZIP         Character    10            N
    6  BEGIN_BAL   Numeric      10      2     N
    7  UPDATE_BAL  Numeric      10      2     N
    8  CR_LIMIT    Numeric      10      2     N
    9  TEXT        Memo         10            N
** Total **                    112
```

Field names → (fields 1–5)

Total number of characters in a record

Figure 2-3: New MASTER File Record Structure

7. Press **[Alt]-[E]** to open the Exit menu.
8. Since you did not change anything, type **A** to select **Abandon changes and exit**.

You are returned to the Control Center.

Using the Go To Record Option

The **Go To** menu in both Edit mode and Browse mode contains options to allow you to position an internal database pointer to a particular record. You can choose to place the pointer at the "Top record" of the file, or the "Last record" of the file, or on any record in between by using "Record number." If you choose Record number, the program will ask you for the number of the specific record at which to place the pointer.

You can use the Go To menu when you want to move to a particular record in a database and modify or view that record. For example, you may want to display a record to see what it contains, or you may want to edit the record to change or correct some of the information in it.

Editing Record Contents

To change the contents of any or all parts of a record, you may use either Edit mode or Browse mode. When you invoke either one, the cursor will be placed on the record where the internal pointer is positioned.

If the internal pointer is not positioned at the record you want to modify, you can reposition it by using one of two methods:

1.   You can either use the Go To menu, or
2.   A.   In Edit mode you can use the **[PgUp]** or **[PgDn]** key to position the pointer to display the record you wish to edit.
      B.   In Browse mode you can use the up arrow [↑] or down arrow [↓] key to position the pointer on the record you wish to edit.

The Go To menu is the best way to position the pointer if the desired record is many (15 or more) records away from the present pointer location.

In the following exercise, you will add comments to the new memo fields of all of your records in the MASTER file, as shown in Table 2-1. Because you will be editing all records, you can begin with record 1 in the file by using Top record in the Go To menu.

To add the comments,

1.   Position the highlight on top of MASTER and press **[Enter]**.
2.   Press **D** to pick Display data.
      If you are in Browse mode (look at the left end of the Status Bar), press **[F2]** to switch into Edit mode.
3.   Type **[Alt]-[G]** to open the **Go To** menu.

Record Num	Memo Field Contents
1	ALWAYS PAYS PROMPTLY.
2	CREDIT IS EXCELLENT. NEVER USES FULL CREDIT LIMIT.
3	CREDIT IS GOOD. SLOW BUT STEADY PAY OFF.
4	ACTIVE CREDIT USER. ALWAYS CHARGES WITH CARD, BUT SLOW TO PAY OFF.
5	BAD CREDIT RISK! FOLLOW UP!

Table 2-1: *Comments for Memo Fields*

4.   Either type a **T**, or highlight **Top record** (as shown in Figure 2-4) and press **[Enter]**.

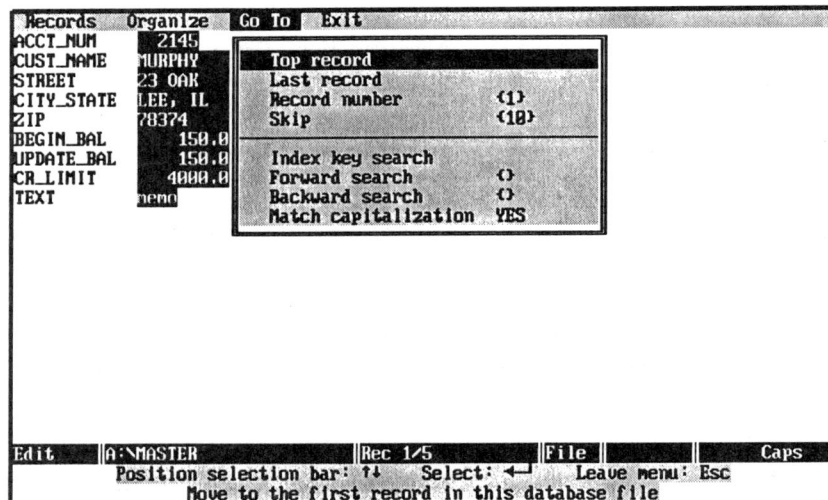

Figure 2-4:
*Using the
GoTo Menu*

The Status Bar should now say Rec 1/5 in the third section, meaning that the cursor is on record 1 of the five records.

5.   Move the cursor to the **TEXT** field--notice that the notation in the field is a lower case "memo"--and press **[F9]** to open the text editor screen for entering memo text.

6.   Type **ALWAYS PAYS PROMPTLY** (as shown in Figure 2-5) for record 1.

7.   Press **[F9]** again to close the edit screen.
Note that the word "MEMO" has changed to uppercase, signifying that text now exists in the memo field for this record.

8.   Press **[PgDn]** to move to the next record.

9.   Repeat steps 5-8 as many times as necessary to complete all of the entries as displayed in Table 2-1.

When you have finished entering the memo comments,

10.   Press **[Alt]-[E]** to open the Exit menu, then **E** to Exit to the Control Center.

NOTE: Should you press [PgDn] while on record 5, dBASE will ask "Add new records? (Y/N)." Type N to move back to record 5 without adding any new records.

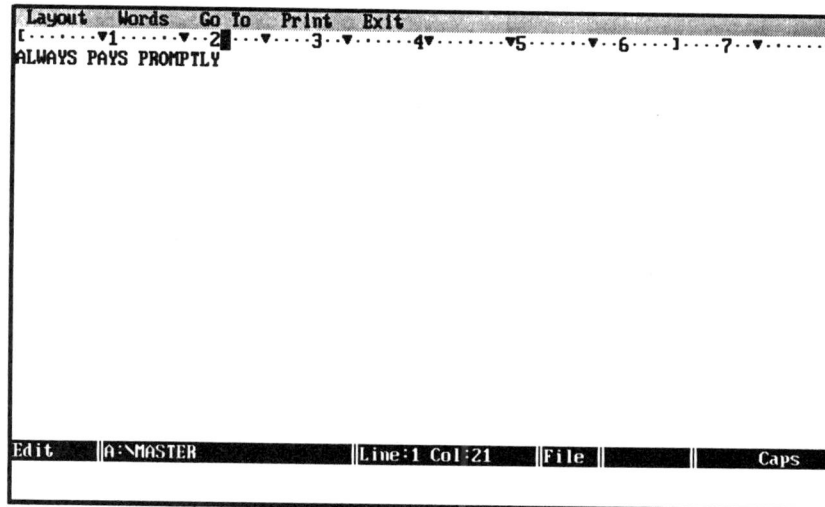

```
 Layout   Words   Go To   Print   Exit
[·······▼1·····▼··2█···▼····3··▼·····4▼·····▼5·····▼··6···]···7··▼·····
ALWAYS PAYS PROMPTLY




















 Edit   ║A:\MASTER          ║Line:1 Col:21║    ║File║           ║    Caps
```

Figure 2-5: *Entering Memo Text*

Field Name	Record 1	Record 2	Record 3
ACCT_NUM	4140	411	2118
CUST_NAME	HENDERSON	TORREY	MOLANDER
STREET	605 3RD	PO BOX 2	1620 BROADWAY
CITY_STATE	NEWARK, NJ	FIELDS, OR	SEATTLE, WA
ZIP	01954	97837	98031
BEGIN_BAL	150.00	200.00	300.00
UP-DATE_BAL	0.00	0.00	300.00
CR_LIMIT	6000.00	2000.00	1000.00
TEXT	EXCELLENT	SLOW TO PAY	POOR RISK!

Table 2-2: *Additional MASTER File Records*

Using Browse Mode to Append

In the following exercise, you will use Browse mode to add the additional records shown in Table 2-2 to the database MASTER. To add the three records, place the highlight bar on top of MASTER, and

1. Press **[Enter]**.
2. Type **D** to Display data.
3. If the Status Bar says Edit at the left end, press **[F2]** to switch into Browse mode.
4. Move the cursor toward the bottom of the screen (with the down arrow **[↓]**) until the following prompt appears below the status bar (as shown in Figure 2-6),

   Add new records? [Y/N]

   In response to the prompt,
5. Press **Y**.

Records	Organize	Fields	Go To	Exit	

ACCT_NUM	CUST_NAME	STREET	CITY_STATE	ZIP
2145	MURPHY	23 OAK	LEE, IL	78374
4115	ADAMS	412 ELM	MAR, CA	95485
4155	JONES	345 ELM	LEE, IL	78374
6598	MCCLURE	986 OAK	LEE, IL	78374
6155	ODEGARD	98 ELM	OAK, CA	96254

Browse	A:\MASTER	Rec 5/5	File	

===> Add new records? (Y/N)

Figure 2-6:
Adding New
Records

In the first field,
6. Type **4140** and press **[Enter]**.
   The cursor will move to the next highlighted field, as shown in Figure 2-7.
7. Type **HENDERSON** and press **[Enter]**.
8. Type **605 3RD** and press **[Enter]**.
9. Type **NEWARK, NJ** and press **[Enter]**.
10. Type **01954** and press **[Enter]**.
11. Type **150** and press **[Enter]**.
12. Type **0** and press **[Enter]**.
13. Type **6000** and press **[Enter]**.
14. Press **[F9]** at the memo field and type **EXCELLENT**.
15. Press **[F9]** to leave the memo editor screen.
16. Press **[Enter]** to move to the beginning of another new record.
17. Add the remaining records of Table 2-2 using steps 6 through 16. To stop adding new records, end Browse mode, and exit to the Control Center,
18. Press **[Alt]-[E]** to open the Exit menu,

```
 Records   Organize   Fields   Go To   Exit
 ACCT_NUM│CUST_NAME          │STREET          │CITY_STATE  │ZIP
     2145│MURPHY             │23 OAK          │LEE, IL     │78374
     4115│ADAMS              │412 ELM         │MAR, CA     │95485
     4155│JONES              │345 ELM         │LEE, IL     │78374
     6598│MCCLURE            │986 OAK         │LEE, IL     │78374
     6155│ODEGARD            │98 ELM          │OAK, CA     │96254
     4140│                   │                │            │

 Browse   │A:\MASTER              │Rec EOF/5      │File │            │    Caps
                                 Add new records
```

Figure 2-7:
*Appending a
Record on
the Browse
Screen*

19.   Press **E** to Exit.

Using Searching to Locate a Record to Edit

During the time that a business exists, its customer information will
very likely undergo changes. Consequently the data in their files must
be altered to reflect these changes, changes that might include such
things as new addresses, changes in credit limits, or name changes.
Both Edit mode and Browse mode allow you to move to any field within
a record and change the data in that field. You may type over the
existing data or press the **[Insert]** key and insert characters, as well as
delete characters with the **[Delete]** key. In the following exercise, you
will make the changes shown in Table 2-3.

As a database grows, it can reach hundreds or thousands of records.
It would be impractical to read every record searching for the correct
record to edit. The Go To menu contains Forward search and Backward search to have dBASE IV search for you. Both search directions
will locate the proper record; the only difference is in which direction
they begin looking. Forward means searching from the current record
toward the bottom of the database then wrapping back to the top until
returning to the current record; Backward begins toward the top and
wraps back onto the bottom. Searching **must** begin with the cursor in
the field you are searching on.

Customer Number	Field	New Information
4115	CUST_NAME	BROWN
6155	STREET	2150 MAIN STREET

Table 2-3: *MASTER File Record Updates*

To change the data in the two records and use searching to locate the proper listings, make sure that the highlight bar is on top of MASTER, and

1. Press **[Enter]**.
2. Type **D** to Display data.
3. If necessary, press **[F2]** to switch to Edit mode.
    To search for account number 4115, be sure the cursor is in the ACCT_NUM field, and
4. Press **[Alt]-[G]** to open the GoTo menu.
5. Type an **F** to begin a Forward search.
6. In the Enter search string box, type **4115** (as shown in Figure 2-8) and press **[Enter]**.
    The correct record (ADAMS) should appear.

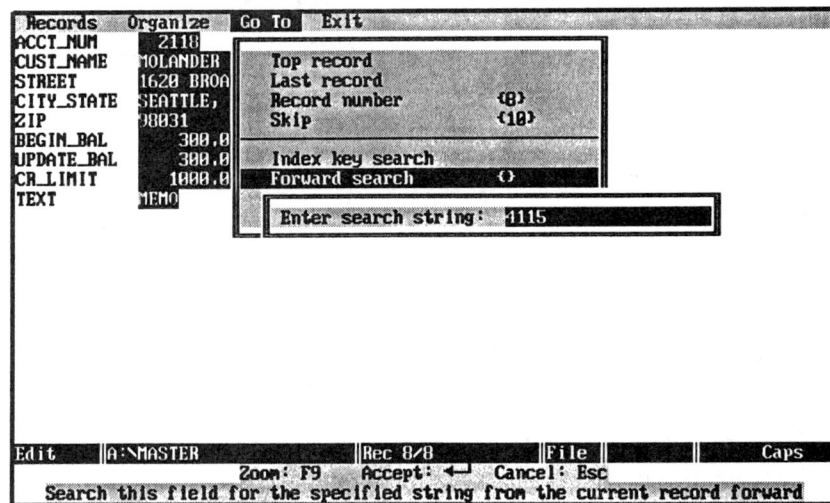

Figure 2-8:
Searching on the Edit Screen

Move the cursor down to the beginning of the CUST_NAME field, and

7. Type **BROWN** and press **[Enter]**.
    Remembering that you must have the cursor in the field you are searching on, move up to ACCT_NUM again.
8. Press **[Alt]-[G]** to open the GoTo menu.
9. Type an **F** to begin a Forward search.
10. In the Enter search string box, backspace over the old **4115** value and type **6155**, and press **[Enter]**.
    The correct record (ODEGARD) should appear.
    Move the cursor down to the beginning of the STREET field, and,
11. Type **2150 MAIN STREET** and press **[Enter]**.
    To view the changes to the database file,
12. Switch into Browse mode by pressing **[F2]**.
13. Press **[Alt]-[E]** to open the Exit menu.
14. Press **E** to Exit to the Control Center.

Editing in Browse Mode

Editing in Browse mode is exactly the same as in Edit mode. You locate the record, then change the data. For example, if Brown has moved to 100 Elm, you search for the name BROWN, then type 100 ELM over the old address. Since you are now searching for a **name,** be sure that you move the cursor into the CUST_NAME field, and that you type BROWN in uppercase in the following exercise. (Uppercase is mandatory if "Match capitalization," the last item in the menu, says YES).

To view MASTER,

1. Press **[Enter]** and type **D** to Display data.
2. Use the **[Enter]** or **[Tab]** key to move to the CUST_NAME field. To search on this field,
3. Press **[Alt]-[G]** to open the Go To menu and type **F** to begin a Forward search.
4. Type **BROWN** in the Enter search string box, and press **[Enter]**.
5. Press **[Tab]** to move over to the ADDRESS field, as shown in Figure 2-9.

Figure 2-9:
Editing on the Browse Screen

Records	Organize	Fields	Go To	Exit		

ACCT_NUM	CUST_NAME	STREET	CITY_STATE	ZIP
4115	BROWN	412 ELM	MAR, CA	95485
4155	JONES	345 ELM	LEE, IL	78374
6598	MCCLURE	986 OAK	LEE, IL	78374
6155	ODEGARD	2150 MAIN STREET	OAK, CA	96254
4140	HENDERSON	685 3RD	NEWARK, NJ	01954
411	TORREY	PO BOX 2	FIELDS, OR	97837
2118	MOLANDER	1620 BROADWAY	SEATTLE, WA	98031

Browse	A:\MASTER		Rec 2/8		File			Caps

6. Type **100** on top of the 412, and press **[Enter]**.

Sometimes, you will know the record number for the record you want to change. To view or edit the data in record 4,

1. Press **[Alt]-[G]** to open the Go To menu and type **R** for Record number.
2. Backspace over any number that may be in the Enter record number box and type **4**, followed by the **[Enter]** key.
    The data should appear showing MCCLURE. The status line confirms that this is record 4 in the file. The data for record 4 is correct, and therefore you do not need to make corrections.

3.   Press **[Alt]-[E]** to open the Exit menu.
4.   Press **E** to Exit to the Control Center.

Deleting Records and Files

There are several ways to delete records from a database file. However, before you use any delete commands, you should understand some of the terminology dBASE IV uses with regard to deleting records. When you issue a delete command for a record, the program considers the record to be "marked for deletion," but does not physically delete it from the database. You can therefore recall deleted records, which means that their "marks for deletion" can be removed.

Because the records that are marked for deletion are actually still in the file, a database file that accumulates many deleted records takes up excessive file space on the disk. You can clean up such a file by "packing." Packing means that records not marked for deletion are copied to another file, the original database file is erased, and the new file is renamed to the original file name. This process may take several minutes for large database files, but the command to do this is simple to use.

Deleting a Single Record

To delete a single record, you can position the record pointer on that record and use the "Mark record for deletion" menu choice. Suppose you want to delete the record for customer Torrey. You can locate the record by searching.

In the following exercise, you will delete the record for TORREY. First, however, you will back up your database file and add the backup to the catalog. To do so,

1.   Type **[Alt]-[T]** to open the Tools menu.
2.   Select **DOS utilities** by pressing **D**.
      On the DOS util screen, in the file listings notice that there are four MASTER files: your database is MASTER.DBF, and its memo file is MASTER.DBT. Both of these must be copied. The other two files MASTER.DBK and MASTER.TBK are left over from the changes you made to the structure of MASTER. They are outdated files and can be ignored.
      To copy more than one file with a single copy command, mark the files by moving the highlight on top of the filename and pressing **[Enter]**. A triangle will indicate that the name has been marked, and the copy operation can apply to all marked files.
3.   Move the highlight on top of **MASTER.DBF** and press **[Enter]** to mark the name.
4.   Move the highlight on top of **MASTER.DBT** and press **[Enter]** to mark that name (as shown in Figure 2-10).
5.   Press **[Alt]-[O]** to open the Operations menu.
6.   Press **C** to select **Copy**.

7. Type **M** to choose **Marked Files** since you want to copy both
    marked files.

    In the resulting dialog box under the word **Copy** it should say
    "All <marked> files in current directory." The Drive:Directory
    should say A:.

8. Press **[Enter]** to move over to the Filename section.

9. Type **MASTERBU.***, as shown in Figure 2-11.

    The asterisk means to use the same extensions as the original
    files.

10. Press **[Ctrl]-[End]** as prompted in the navigation line at the
    bottom of the screen to perform the copy.

    The screen display will be redrawn and both MASTERBU.DBF
    and MASTERBU.DBT should be listed.

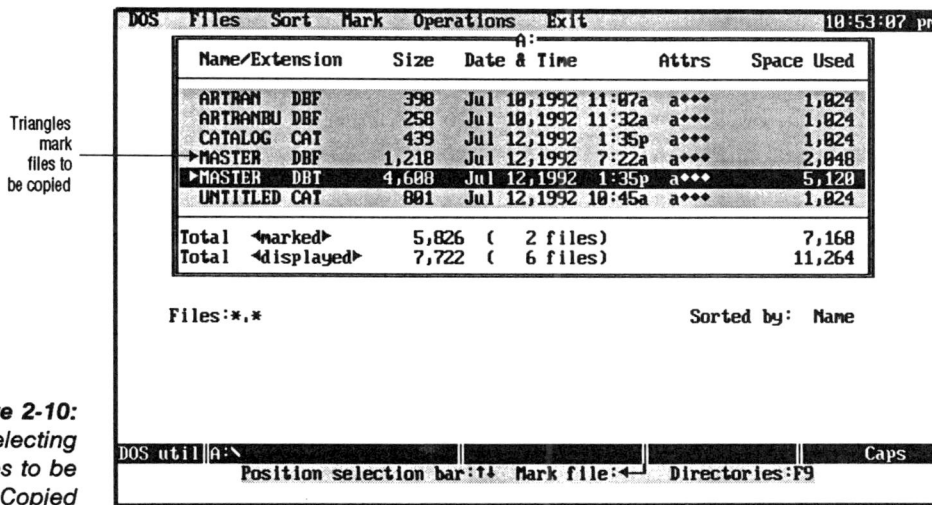

Triangles
mark
files to
be copied

Figure 2-10:
Selecting
Files to be
Copied

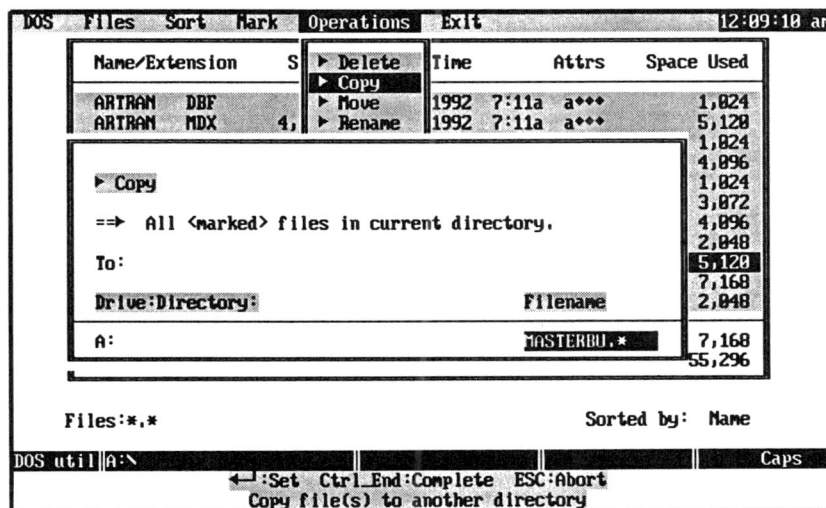

Figure 2-11:
Entering the
New
Filename

11.   Press **[Alt]-[E]** to open the Exit menu and select **Exit to Control Center**.

To add MASTERBU to the catalog,

1.   Be sure that the highlight is in the Data panel.
2.   Press **[Alt]-[C]** to open the Catalog menu.
3.   Select **Add file to catalog** by pressing **A**.
     A list of the available database files on the active disk will appear.
4.   Move the highlight bar on top of **MASTERBU.DBF** and press **[Enter]**.
     A box for editing the description of the file appears. To specify the description,
5.   Type **BACKUP OF MASTER FILE** and press **[Enter]**.

To delete Torrey,

1.   With the highlight bar on top of MASTER, press **[Enter]**.
2.   Type **D** to pick Display data.
3.   If necessary, press **[F2]** to switch to Edit mode to better distinguish one record from the next.
4.   Press **[Tab]** to move into the CUST_NAME field.
5.   Type **[Alt]-[G]** to open the Go To menu.
6.   Press **F** for Forward search.
7.   Type **TORREY** in the Enter search string box, and press **[Enter]**.
     The record pointer is now located on the appropriate record. You can now delete the record.
8.   Type **[Alt]-[R]** to open the Records menu.
9.   Press **M** to pick **Mark record for deletion** (as shown in Figure 2-12).
     The "marked for deletion" indicator is the **Del** in the last section of the Status Bar (as shown in Figure 2-13).
10.   Press **[PgUp]** to move to record 6 and note that there is no **Del** marker since that record has not been marked for deletion.

In the following exercise, you will delete the first record in the database file.

1.   Type **[Alt]-[G]** to open the Go To menu and press **T** for Top record.
     The Status Bar should show Rec 1/8 and the name should be MURPHY.
2.   Type **[Alt]-[R]** to open the Records menu and press **M** to pick **Mark record for deletion**.
     Two records are now marked for deletion.

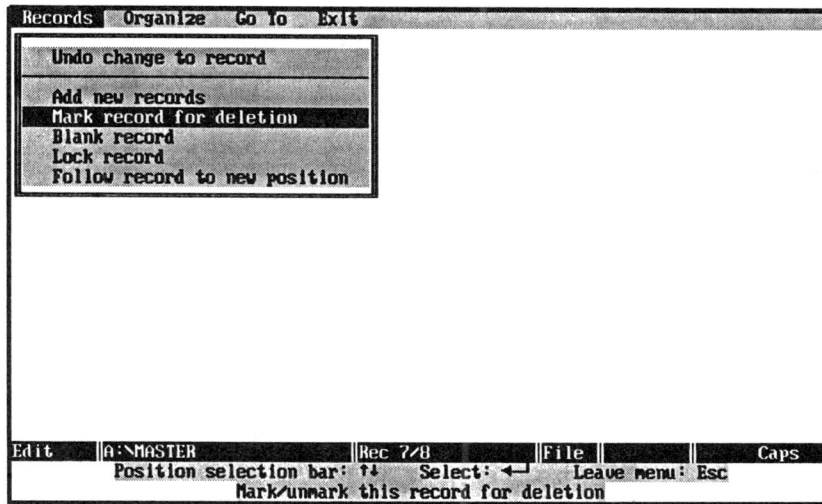

Figure 2-12:
Marking
Records for
Deletion

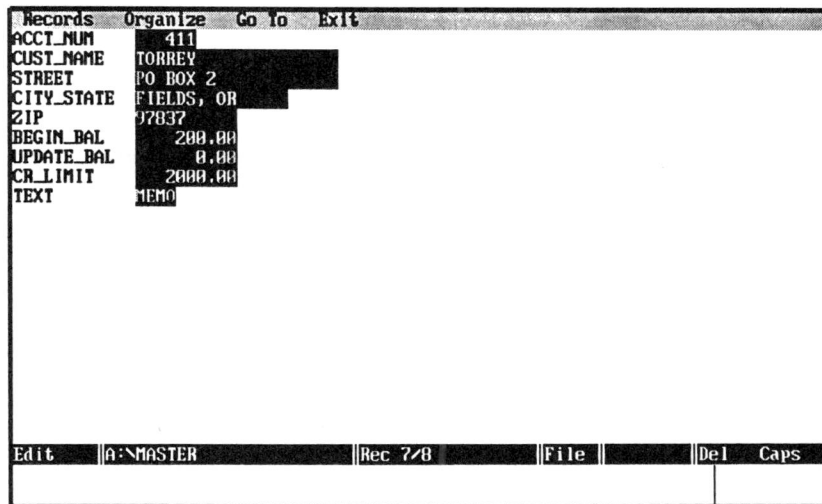

Figure 2-13:
The Delete
Marker

The
delete
marker

If you accidentally mark the wrong record for deletion or you change your mind, you can remove the Del by using the "Clear deletion mark" selection in the Records menu. This selection appears only when the cursor is on a record that is marked for deletion.

To unmark (that is, undelete) record 1,

1. Press **[Alt]-[R]** to open the Records menu.
2. Type **C** to pick Clear deletion mark.
    The Del should disappear from the Status Bar.

As previously mentioned, a database file may eventually contain many deleted records. To remove these records physically from the database file,

1. Press **[Alt]-[O]** to open the Organize menu.
2. Type **E** to choose **Erase marked records** (as shown in Figure 2-14).

Figure 2-14:
Erasing the Marked Records

3. Answer "Are you sure you want to erase all marked records?" by pressing **Y** for Yes.

A message indicates that seven records were copied during the PACK operation. Since you had eight records before the deletion, one record must have been erased. Had more than one record been marked, all of the marked records would have been erased.

To verify that TORREY was erased,
1. Press the down arrow [↓] to move into the CUST_NAME field.
2. Type **[Alt]-[G]** to open the Go To menu.
3. Press **F** for Forward search.
4. TORREY should still be in the Enter search string box, so just press **[Enter]**. (If not, type TORREY and press [Enter].) The message "** Not Found **" should appear (as shown in Figure 2-15). TORREY no longer exists within the database file. There is no way to bring the deleted record back except to retype the data, or use a backup copy of the database.
5. Press any key as noted in the message box.

You have completed the last exercise in Lesson 2. At this point, you can either quit or go on to the review exercises. If you decide to quit, remember that you must exit properly to ensure that all files are correctly closed; failure to close the files before turning the computer off can result in loss of data!

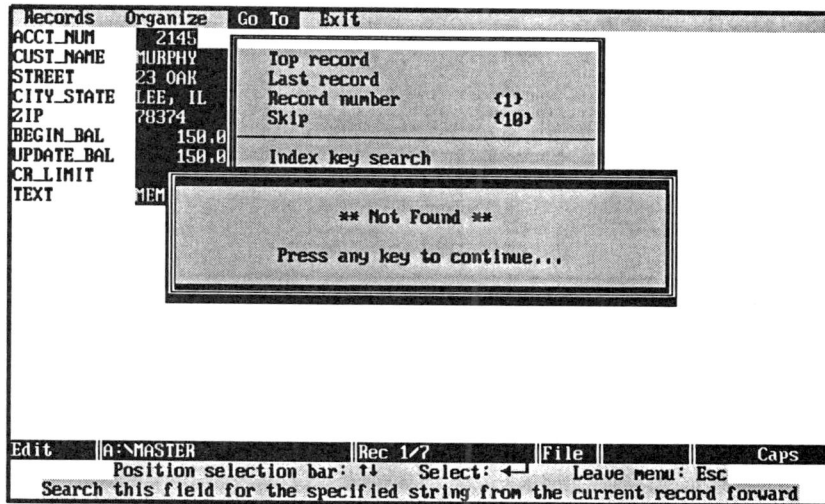

Figure 2-15:
Confirming
the Record
was Erased

Review Exercises

1. List the steps for retrieving files in the ASSIST mode.
    Practice retrieving files using these steps.
2. List the steps for modifying a record structure to add a field and to change a field's width.
3. List the steps for positioning the pointer to a particular record.
4. List the steps necessary to add one record to a file using Browse mode.
5. List the steps necessary to edit one record in a file using Browse mode.
6. Perform the following tasks to modify the name and address file, PRAC1, that you created in Lesson 1:
    A. Add a telephone number field to the file.
    B. Print the new structure.
    C. Enter telephone numbers for each of the five records in your file.
    D. Use the GOTO option to position the pointer at record 3. Change the person's name in record 3.
    E. Use Browse mode to add two new records to the file.
    F. Mark for deletion the first of your two new records and then erase the record.
    G. View all of the records in the file to confirm that it was erased.

3

Querying a Database

The objectives of this lesson are to
- ▶ Create a query
- ▶ Select fields for inclusion in the view
- ▶ Display the resulting view
- ▶ Use multiple criteria in a query

Creating a Query

In working with databases you often need to select only certain records that match some specifications. Perhaps you need a list of those customers whose balances are at their credit limit. To obtain such a specific listing in dBASE IV, you perform a query.

Query is the formal term for searching a database for all records that match some criterion. Sample criteria might be "all customers who live in New York" or "any account more than 30 days overdue."

dBASE IV uses "query by example." That means, rather than type out a lengthy command for the criterion, you simply fill in a diagram of the database structure with an example of what you are trying to match.

Besides merely searching for matches, a query can also select which fields should be included in the answer.

The resulting answer is called a "view." In addition to seeing the data, a view can be used to create reports or labels, and (for simple queries) may be edited.

In the following exercises you will build several varieties of queries.

To create a query that searches MASTER,

1.   Open the MASTER database for use. (If necessary, review the procedure for opening a file in Lesson 1.)
      MASTER should appear above the horizontal line in the Data panel.
2.   Press the right arrow [→] to move the highlight bar onto <create> in the Queries panel (as shown in Figure 3-1), and press **[Enter]**.

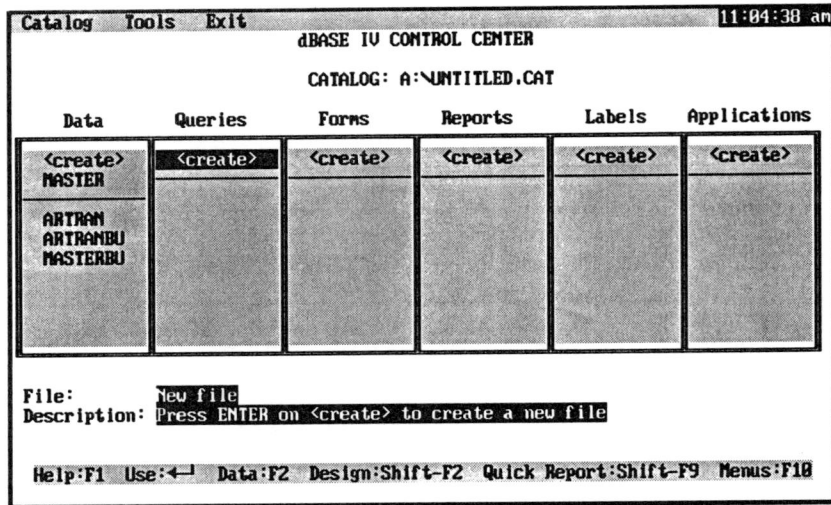

Figure 3-1:
Creating a
Query

The Query screen will appear with the "file skeleton" for MASTER at
the top of the screen and the file skeleton for the view just above the
Status Bar (as shown in Figure 3-2). A file skeleton is a diagram of the
structure of the named file. The name of the file is at the left end of the
skeleton. Each field of MASTER is represented and named in its own
section of the file skeleton.

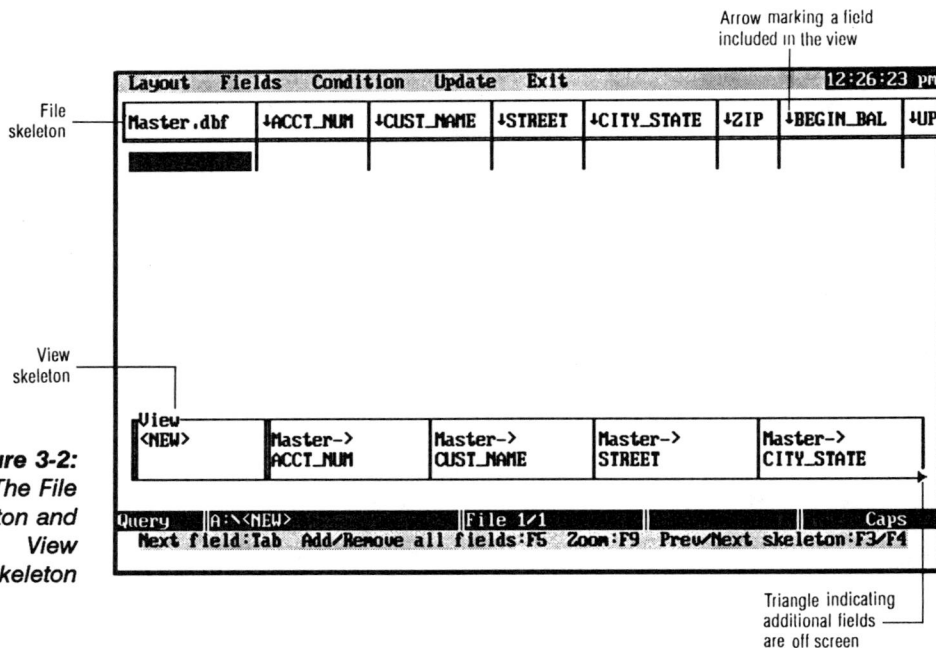

Figure 3-2:
The File
Skeleton and
View
Skeleton

When a database is open at the time a query is created, every field is
automatically included in the view. A downward pointing arrow in a
field shows that that field has been included. If the **[F5]** key is pressed

while under the filename (Master.dbf in this example), it will remove all fields from the view or include all fields in the view. If pressed while in an individual field, only that single field will be removed from or included in the view. Thus, any combination of fields can be obtained in the view. Only those fields in the view skeleton will be included in the answer.

To move to any field in the skeleton, press the **[Tab]** or **[Shift]-[Tab]** keys, as noted in the navigation line.

To query for all records that have an updated balance of less than $300,

```
Layout   Fields   Condition   Update   Exit                    12:28:29 pm
┌─────────┬────────┬───────────┬─────┬───────────┬────────────┬──────────┬──┐
│Master.dbf│↓STREET │↓CITY_STATE│↓ZIP │↓BEGIN_BAL │↓UPDATE_BAL │↓CR_LIMIT │↓T│
├─────────┴────────┴───────────┴─────┴───────────┼────────────┼──────────┴──┤
│         │        │           │     │           │<300        │             │
│                                                                            │
│                                                                            │
│                                                                            │
│ ┌View────┬─────────┬─────────┬─────────┬──────────┐                        │
│ │<NEW>   │Master-> │Master-> │Master-> │Master->  │                        │
│ │        │ACCT_NUM │CUST_NAME│STREET   │CITY_STATE│                        │
└─┴────────┴─────────┴─────────┴─────────┴──────────┴───────────────────────┘
Query    A:\<NEW>              Field 7/9                            Caps
    Prev/Next field:Shift-Tab/Tab  Data:F2  Size:Shift-F7  Prev/Next skel:F3/F4
```

Figure 3-3: Editing the Criterion

1. Press **[Tab]** to move to the UPDATE_BAL field.
2. Type **<300** and press **[Enter]** (as shown in Figure 3-3).
3. Press the **[F2]** key to see the result of the query on the Edit or Browse screen.
   As you are interested in seeing all of the matching answers at once, switch to the Browse screen, if necessary. Two listings (MURPHY and HENDERSON) from the seven in the database should appear.
   To confirm that they have an updated balance lower than $300,
4. Press **[Tab]** until the UPDATE_BAL field appears.
   You can reuse the same query by transferring back to the query design screen and changing the criteria, then viewing the new answer. That way, many different views can be examined quickly.
   To change the query,
5. Press **[Alt]-[E]** to open the Exit menu.
6. Type **T** to pick Transfer to Query Design.

You had to tab over to the updated balance field to confirm the listings in the answer. You probably don't need all of the fields from

MASTER in the view. To select only certain fields, add or remove them with the **[F5]** key. To include only the ACCT_NUM, CUST_NAME, and UPDATE_BAL fields,

1. Press **[Home]** to jump to the beginning of the file skeleton (under the name Master.dbf).
2. Press **[F5]** to remove all fields from the view skeleton.
3. Press **[Tab]** to move to ACCT_NUM.
4. Press **[F5]** to begin the view with ACCT_NUM.
5. Press **[Tab]** to move to CUST_NAME.
6. Press **[F5]** to include CUST_NAME in the view.
7. Press **[Tab]** several times until you get to UPDATE_BAL.
8. Press **[F5]** to include UPDATE_BAL in the view.
   The <300 is still in the UPDATE_BAL field since you still want to limit the listings to those with an updated balance below $300.
9. Press **[F2]** (as noted in the navigation line) to see the view. Only the three specified fields appear for the two selected records (as shown in Figure 3-4).
10. Press **[Alt]-[E]** to open the Exit menu and **T** to transfer back to the query design.

```
 Records   Organize   Fields   Go To   Exit
┌────────────────────────────────────────────────────────────────────┐
│ACCT_NUM│CUST_NAME        │UPDATE_BAL                                 │
├────────┼─────────────────┼───────────────────────────────────────── │
│   2145 │MURPHY           │       150.00                              │
│   4140 │HENDERSON        │         0.00                              │
│        │                 │                                           │
│        │                 │                                           │
│        │                 │                                           │
│        │                 │                                           │
│        │                 │                                           │
│        │                 │                                           │
│        │                 │                                           │
│        │                 │                                           │
│        │                 │                                           │
│        │                 │                                           │
│        │                 │                                           │
│        │                 │                                           │
 Browse  │A:\<NEW>         │        │Rec 1/7      │   │View │    │ Caps
└────────────────────────────────────────────────────────────────────┘
```

Figure 3-4:
The View

You might need other combinations of fields and listings. Since the file skeleton for MASTER is already on the query design screen, you will modify it again for a different problem.

To obtain a list of those customers who live in LEE, IL,

1. Erase the <300 in the UPDATE_BAL field by moving into that field and pressing the **[Del]** key (or the **[Delete]** key) four times.
2. Press **[F5]** in the UPDATE_BAL field to remove it from the view. Only ACCT_NUM and CUST_NAME remain in the view.

3. Press **[Shift]-[Tab]** several times to move to the CITY_STATE field.
4. Press **[F5]** to include it in the view.
5. Type **="LEE, IL"** in the CITY_STATE field as the criterion to be matched (as shown in Figure 3-5).
    Note the quotation marks surrounding the characters in the criterion. Unlike numbers, any data of character type must be surrounded by quotes. (See Table 3-1 for other markers for additional data types.)
6. Move to CR_LIMIT and press **[F5]** to add it to the view.
7. Press **[F2]** to see the results.
    There should be three matches.
8. Press **[Alt]-[E]** to open the Exit menu and **T** to transfer back to the query design.

```
 Layout   Fields   Condition   Update   Exit                    12:45:13 pm
┌─────────────┬────────┬───────────┬─────┬───────────┬────────────┬──────────┬─┐
│ Master.dbf  │ STREET │ ↓CITY_STATE│ ZIP │ BEGIN_BAL │ UPDATE_BAL │ CR_LIMIT │T│
├─────────────┼────────┼───────────┼─────┼───────────┼────────────┼──────────┼─┤
│             │        │ ="LEE, IL"│     │           │            │          │ │
│             │        │           │     │           │            │          │ │
│             │        │           │     │           │            │          │ │
│             │        │           │     │           │            │          │ │
│             │        │           │     │           │            │          │ │
│             │        │           │     │           │            │          │ │
│ ┌View─────────────────────────────────────────────────────────────┐       │
│ │<NEW>     │ Master->   │ Master->    │ Master->                   │       │
│ │          │ ACCT_NUM   │ CUST_NAME   │ CITY_STATE                 │       │
└─┴──────────┴────────────┴─────────────┴────────────────────────────┴───────┘
 Query    A:\<NEW>              Field 4/9                        Caps
    Prev/Next field:Shift-Tab/Tab   Data:F2   Size:Shift-F7   Prev/Next skel:F3/F4
```

Figure 3-5:
The Criterion for a Character Search

Note: If you typed any text into the database using lowercase letters, you must match the case exactly in a query. Only uppercase letters match uppercase; only lowercase matches lowercase. Thus, if you entered the CITY_STATE as "Lee, IL" in the MASTER database file, you must type in mixed case ="Lee, IL" in the query.

Data Type	Delimiting Marks	Example
character	quotes	"NEW YORK"
numeric	none	322.50
date	curly braces	{1/1/93}
logical	periods	.T.

Table 3-1: *Surrounding Markers within Queries*

Along with the two symbols we have already used in queries (> and =), you may use the following:

Symbol	Meaning
=	equal to
>	greater than (after for dates and character data)
<	less than (before for dates and character data)
# or <>	not equal to
>=	greater than or equal to
<=	less than or equal to
$	contains

Table 3-2: The Comparison Operators

The $ may be used to locate any records that contain the characters you specify. The characters to be matched may be anywhere within the field in which you include the criterion. To query for anyone who lives in California, whose abbreviation (CA) is only a portion of the CITY_STATE field,

1. Move back to the CITY_STATE field and delete the current criterion.
2. Type **$"CA"** in the CITY_STATE field as the criterion to be matched (as shown in Figure 3-6).
   Remember, quotation marks must surround character data in the criterion.

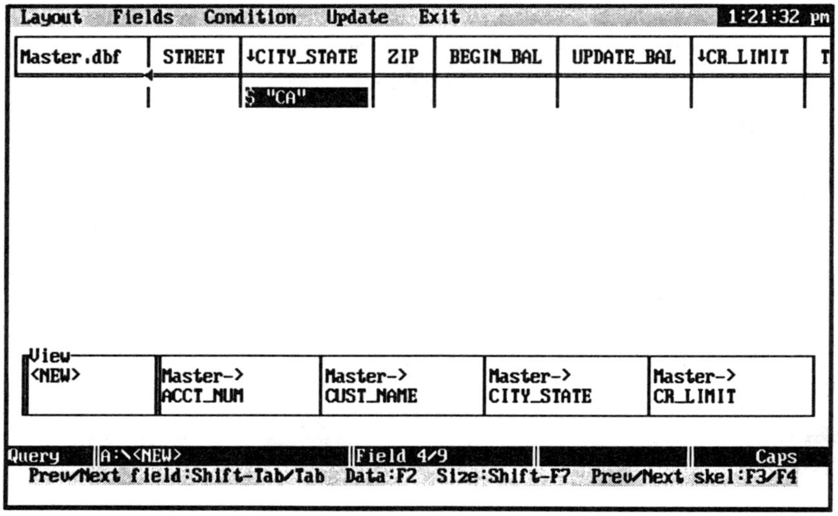

Figure 3-6: The Criterion for a Partial Match

3.　　　Press **[F2]** to see the results.

There should be two matches. Notice that even though the CITY_STATE didn't start with "CA," dBASE found the characters within the field. Had there been a city name containing a "CA" within it, that record would have been included, as well.

4.　　　Press **[Alt]-[E]** to open the Exit menu and **T** to transfer back to the query design.

You are finished with the current query but would like to save it so that you can reuse it at a later time. To exit the query design screen and save the criteria,

1.　　　Press **[Alt]-[E]** to open the Exit menu and **S** to Save changes and exit.

2.　　　Type **CA** in the Save as: box (as shown in Figure 3-7) for the filename by which the query will be recorded on the disk and press **[Enter]**.

Figure 3-7:
Saving the Query

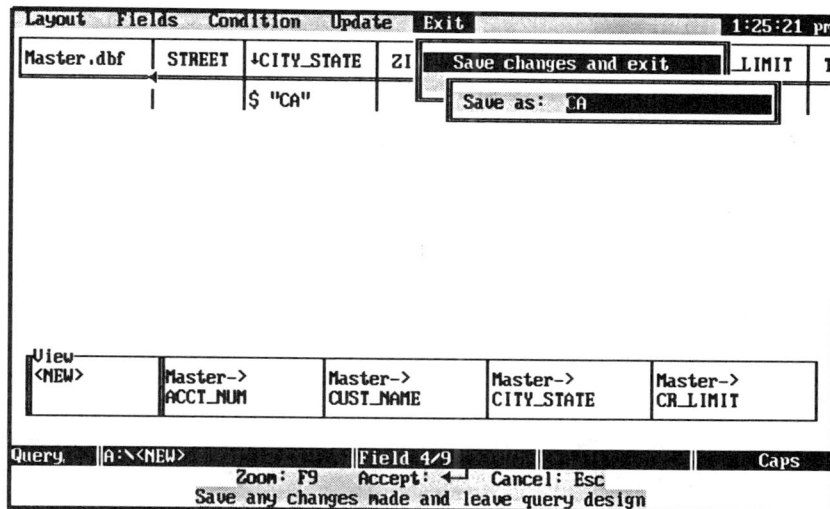

The query name CA appears in the Queries panel. CA is open since it is still above the horizontal line. To close the query, modify the query design, or display the records selected by this query, make certain the highlight is on top of the filename and press **[Enter].** In the resulting dialog box, select the desired choice.

To display the data from the Control Center,

1.　　　Press **[Enter]** when the highlight is on CA.

2.　　　Type **D** to select Display data.

On the display screen, the fourth section of the Status Bar shows that a view is in effect.

3.　　　Use the Exit menu to exit back to the Control Center.

4.   Press **[Enter]** with the highlight on CA, and type **C** to Close the query.

Multiple Criteria in Queries

Many criteria are more complex than just a single match. For example, you might need to find all customers who live in California **and** have an updated balance higher than $500. When you have multiple criteria that are connected with the word AND, that is called an AND query. In dBASE IV, set up an AND query by placing more than one example to be matched (criterion) in a single row of a file skeleton.

The other variety of multiple query is an OR query. An example would be all customers who live in California **or** live in Illinois. dBASE IV implements an OR query by placing criteria in two or more rows of a skeleton.

AND Queries

To query for records in ARTRAN with the DATE equal to 09/17/92 **and** an AMOUNT less than 0 (negative),

1.   Press **[Enter]** with the highlight on top of ARTRAN.
2.   Type **U** to pick Use file.
     The filename moves above the line.
3.   Move the highlight over to <create> in the Queries panel, and press **[Enter]**.
4.   Press **[Tab]** to move to the DATE field.
5.   Type **={9/17/92}** and press **[Enter]**.
     Note that curly braces surround dates in a query.
6.   Press **[Tab]** to move to the AMOUNT field.
7.   Type **<0** and press **[Enter]** (as shown in Figure 3-8).

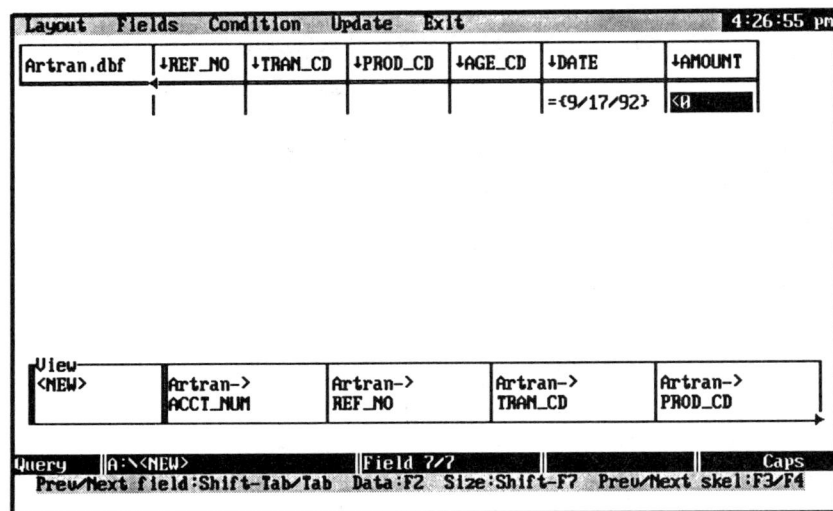

Figure 3-8: Multiple Criteria in an And Query

Since both criteria are in the same row of the query, they must both be true simultaneously, making an AND query.

8.   Press **[F2]** to examine the view.
Only two of the four records in ARTRAN match the double condition of 9/17/92 and AMOUNT less than 0.

9.   Return to the design screen with **[Alt]-[E]** and **T**.
You will not save this query, so

10.   Press **[Alt]-[E]** for the Exit menu and **A** to pick Abandon changes and exit.
To answer "Are you sure you want to abandon operation?"

11.   Type **Y** for Yes.

OR Queries

To query MASTER for customers who live in either California **or** Illinois,

1.   Move the highlight bar onto MASTER, press **[Enter]**, and type **U** to open (use) MASTER.
2.   Move the highlight onto <create> in the Queries panel and press **[Enter]**.
3.   Press **[Tab]** to move to the CITY_STATE field.
4.   Type **$ "CA"** for California.
5.   Press the down arrow [↓] to move onto the second line of the skeleton.
6.   Type **$ "IL"** and press **[Enter]** (as shown in Figure 3-9) to include Illinois.

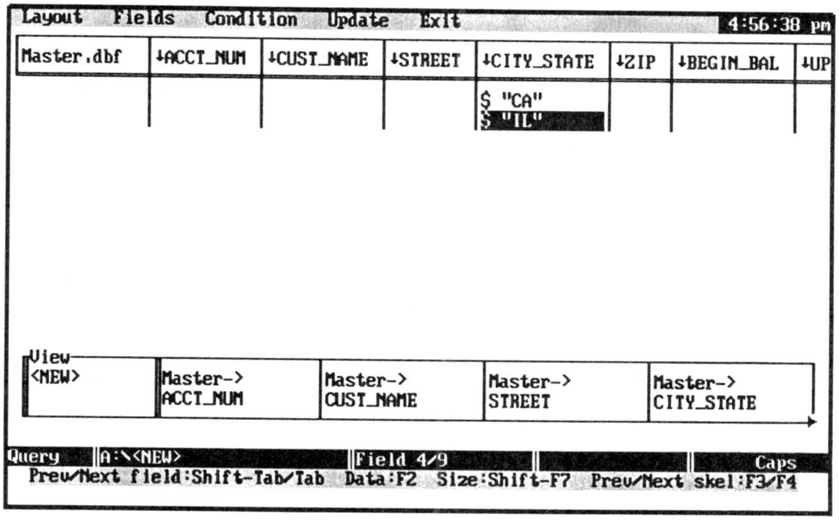

Figure 3-9: Multiple Criteria in an Or Query

7.   Press **[F2]** to see the view. Five of the seven records should appear.

8. Press **[Alt]-[E]** to open the Exit menu and **T** to transfer back to the query design.
9. Press **[Alt]-[E]** to open the Exit menu and **S** to Save changes and exit.
10. Type **IL_OR_CA** in the Save as: box.
11. Close the query by pressing **[Enter]** with the highlight on top of IL_OR_CA and typing **C** to Close.

You have completed the last exercise of Lesson 3 and may now choose to either continue or quit. If you decide to quit, remember to properly exit from the program; failure to close the files before you turn the computer off can result in loss of data!

Review Exercises

1. List the steps necessary to query for all records with an UP-DATE_BAL greater than $300.
2. Using the name and address file, PRAC1, which you modified in the previous lesson,
    A. Add five more records to the file. Enter "NY" or "NEW YORK" into the STATE field for each of the five new records. Enter "KLOVIS" into the CITY field for each of the five new records.
    B. Display all of the records in the file.
    C. Add a new field to the database design to contain entries for an amount due. Name the field AMOUNT_DUE. The field should be large enough to contain a value of $9,999.99.
    D. Print the new file structure.
    E. Enter an amount into the new AMOUNT_DUE field for all of the records in the file, making about half of them larger than $1000, and the remainder smaller than $1000.
    F. Query PRAC1 for all records with an AMOUNT_DUE larger than $1000.
    G. Query PRAC1 for all records in NEW YORK (or NY).
    H. Query PRAC1 for all records with an AMOUNT_DUE smaller than $1000. Include only the person's name, zip code, and amount due.
    I. Query PRAC1 for all records with the AMOUNT_DUE greater than $1000 AND in New York.
    J. Query PRAC 1 for all records with the AMOUNT_DUE greater than $1000 OR in New York.

4

Organizing Database Files

The objectives of this lesson are to
- ▶ Sort on single and multiple fields
- ▶ Index a file
- ▶ Select an index

Organizing Database Files

Up to this point, dBASE IV has stored records in the order in which
you entered them. If you entered them in alphabetical order, the program stored the file in alphabetical order; if not, the file was in random
order. You can change a database file from random to alphabetical,
numeric, or date order by using one of two methods: sorting or indexing.

Sorting creates another file that contains the same data in a different
order. The field you decide to sort will determine the order of the
sorted file. Most often, files containing people's names are sorted by the
last name field, so that the file's records are in alphabetical order by
last name. However, you might also want to sort a file using the ZIP
code field so that mailings can be handled more efficiently.

You can sort fields in either ascending or descending order. Ascending
order is from A to Z, from the lowest number to the highest number (1
to 10), or from earliest date to latest date. Descending order is from Z
to A, from the highest to lowest number (10 to 1), or latest date to
earliest. The default for sorting is ascending order. If there are digits
mixed in with letters (as in product numbers or in addresses), digits
come ahead of letters in ascending order.

One disadvantage to sorting files is that the sorted file is static. This
means that you must perform a new sort each time you add records or
edit the data.

The other way to organize a database is to index it. When you index a
file, you create another file, a file with an .MDX extension, that can be
used with the file whenever needed. Indexing does not change the order
of the file's records the way sorting them does; but rather the records

are "tagged" to appear in a certain order when the index file is active. When you sort a file, the records will only appear in one set order, but you can make up to 47 different indexes for any database file, and switch from one to another.

In this lesson, you will practice both sorting and indexing a file.

Sorting on a Single Field

You will begin by sorting your MASTER file into alphabetical order by name, using commands in the Organize menu. The Organize menu can be found on the Edit screen, the Browse screen, and the Database design screen. To start the sorting procedure,

1.   Display the data in the MASTER file in Browse mode.
2.   Press **[Alt]-[O]** to open the Organize menu.
3.   Type **S** to select Sort database on field list.

dBASE IV opens a "sort box" in which you can fill in the field or combination of fields you wish to sort by, as well as the type of sort. The sort types are Ascending ASCII, Descending ASCII, Ascending Dictionary, and Descending Dictionary. ASCII sorts put all uppercase letters ahead of lowercase letters; Dictionary sorts disregard case. In both types, digits come before letters. Examine Table 4-1 for examples.

Ascending ASCII	Ascending Dictionary
65 Main Street	65 Main Street
Canada	Canada
China	China
United States	china
china	plate
plate	United States

Table 4-1: Sort Order

When the sort box appears (see Figure 4-1),

4.   Press **[Shift]-[F1]** for a "picklist" as mentioned in the Navigation line.
       A picklist contains a listing of all fields from the database. You may press the up arrow [↑] or down arrow [↓] to move the highlight on top of the desired field name and press **[Enter]** to select it. dBASE will then copy that name into the Field order column for you. Of course, you could also type the field name in

the Field order column. The picklist eliminates the need to correctly spell a field name.

5.   Highlight **CUST_NAME** in the picklist (as shown in Figure 4-2)

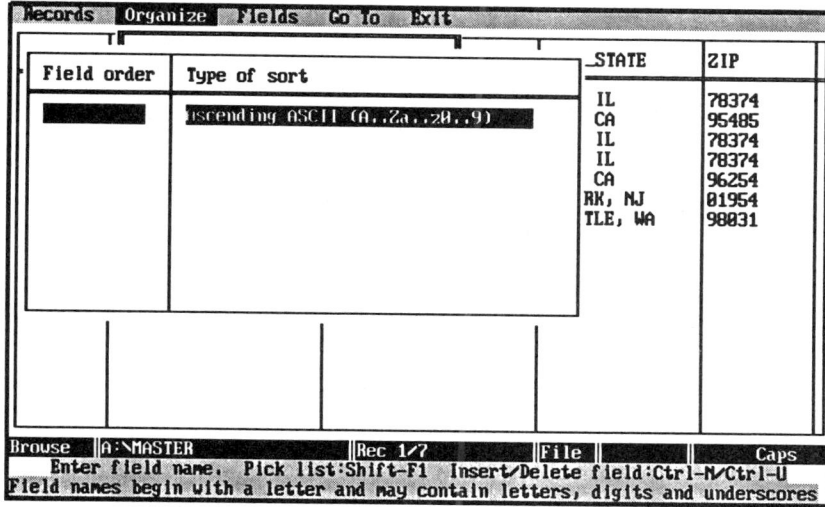

Figure 4-1:
The Sort Box

List
of fields
in the
file

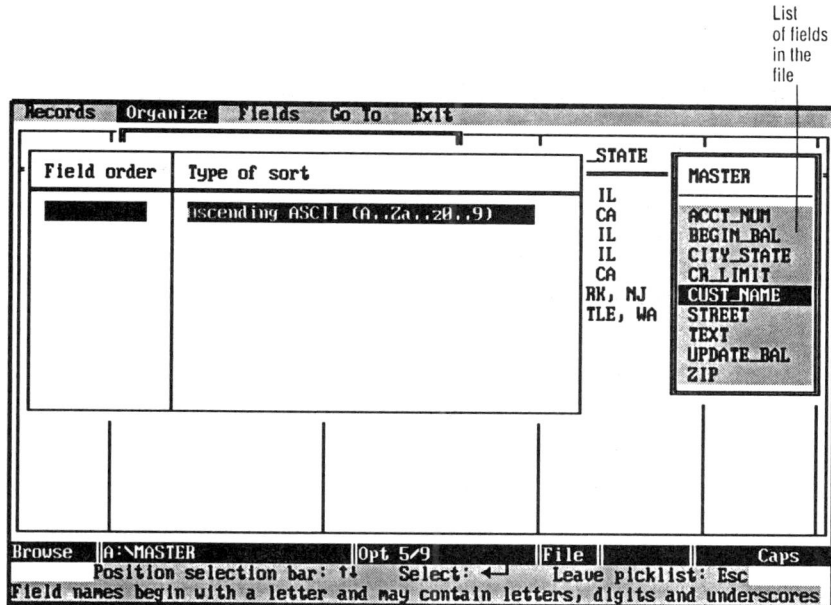

Figure 4-2:
A Picklist

and press **[Enter]**.

6.   Press **[Enter]** to move to the Type of sort column.
          Notice in the Navigation line that each press of the space bar will change to the next type, then

7.   Press **[Enter]** to keep Ascending ASCII as the sort type.
          Since that is the only field you need to sort by,

8. Press **[Ctrl]-[End]** to save and exit.

   Since dBASE will only sort to a new copy of the database, you must supply a new database filename. In the Enter name of sorted file: box,

9. Type **RECSORT1** (as shown on Figure 4-3) and press **[Enter]**. You will see several messages as the sort progresses, and then dBASE will ask for a description. To enter the description,

10. Type **MASTER SORTED BY CUSTOMER NAME** (as shown in Figure 4-4) and press **[Enter]**.

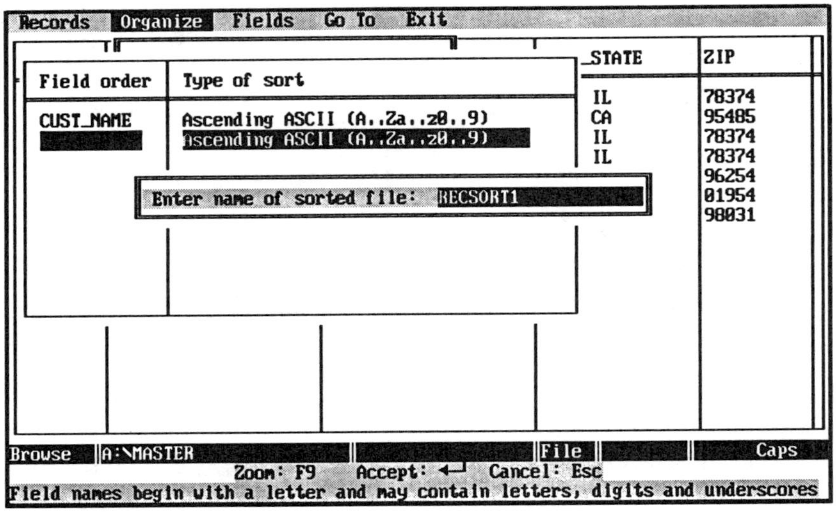

Figure 4-3:
Naming the New File

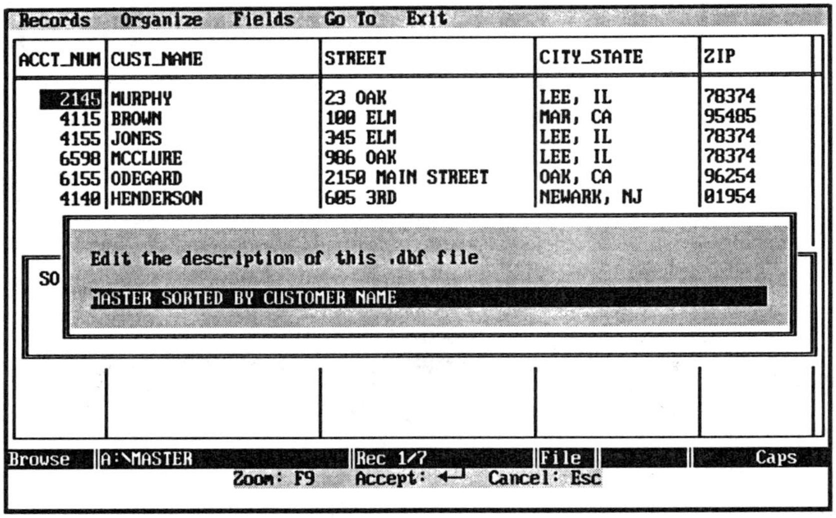

Figure 4-4:
Entering the File Description

The new file RECSORT1 containing the sorted names now exists, but MASTER is still on the screen. To examine the file that contains the sorted records,

1. Press **[Alt]-[E]** for the Exit menu, and **E** to pick Exit.
2. Highlight RECSORT1 in the Data panel and press **[Enter]**.
3. Type **D** to Display data.

The sorted file will appear on the screen. Note that the records are listed in alphabetical order by the customer's last name, as shown in Figure 4-5.

4. Open the Exit menu and pick Exit to return to the Control Center.

Records	Organize	Fields	Go To	Exit		

ACCT_NUM	CUST_NAME	STREET	CITY_STATE	ZIP
4115	BROWN	100 ELM	MAR, CA	95485
4140	HENDERSON	605 3RD	NEWARK, NJ	01954
4155	JONES	345 ELM	LEE, IL	78374
6590	MCCLURE	986 OAK	LEE, IL	78374
2118	MOLANDER	1620 BROADWAY	SEATTLE, WA	98031
2145	MURPHY	23 OAK	LEE, IL	78374
6155	ODEGARD	2150 MAIN STREET	OAK, CA	96254

| Browse | A:\RECSORT1 | | Rec 1/7 | | File | | Caps |

Figure 4-5:
The File Sorted by Customer Name

Sorting on Multiple Fields

You can have a file sorted by more than one field at a time. Often a file is sorted on both the last name and first name fields so that the names are in alphabetical order even when the database file contains several records with the same last name. You could also have the file sorted by the customers' names within the same ZIP code. To sort your MASTER file by both the ZIP and CUST_NAME fields,

1. Place the highlight bar on top of MASTER and press **[Enter]**.
2. Type **D** to select Display data.
3. Open the Organize menu and pick Sort database on field list.
4. Press **[Shift]-[F1]** to open the pick list, and select **ZIP**.
   Since you want Ascending ASCII, which is already showing,
5. Press the down arrow **[↓]** to move to the second line.
6. Press **[Shift]-[F1]** to open the pick list, and select **CUST_NAME**.
   Again, you want Ascending ASCII, so
7. Press **[Ctrl]-[End]** to begin sorting.
8. Type **RECSORT2** and press **[Enter]** to name the file in the Enter name of sorted file: box.
   Following the various messages about sorting,

9. Fill in the description **MASTER SORTED BY ZIP AND CUS-TOMER NAME** and press **[Enter]**.

10. Return to the Control Center.

To examine the file that contains the sorted records,

1. Highlight RECSORT2 in the Data panel and press **[Enter]**.

2. Type **D** to Display data.

The sorted file will appear on the screen. Note how the file is sorted on both the ZIP code and customer name fields (as shown in Figure 4-6, which lists the customers' names in alphabetical order for each ZIP code).

3. Open the Exit menu and pick Exit to return to the Control Center.

Records	Organize	Fields	Go To	Exit

ACCT_NUM	CUST_NAME	STREET	CITY_STATE	ZIP
4140	HENDERSON	605 3RD	NEWARK, NJ	01954
4155	JONES	345 ELM	LEE, IL	78374
6598	MCCLURE	986 OAK	LEE, IL	78374
2145	MURPHY	23 OAK	LEE, IL	78374
4115	BROWN	100 ELM	MAR, CA	95485
6155	ODEGARD	2150 MAIN STREET	OAK, CA	96254
2118	MOLANDER	1620 BROADWAY	SEATTLE, WA	98031

Browse	A:\RECSORT2	Rec 1/7	File		Caps

Figure 4-6:
Sorting by
Zip Code
and Custom-
er Name

Creating Indexes

In addition to organizing a database by sorting it, you can organize records by indexing the database. Unlike the SORT command, the INDEX command creates a file that maintains the database in logical order even when new records are added. One advantage of indexing is that when records are added, deleted, or edited, index files provide automatic updating. Thus, an index file makes the database file appear to be in a specified order when it is displayed. Because this manipulation is done in RAM, it does not affect the physical order of the database.

Additionally, you may create many indexes (up to 47), and indexes can be turned on and off as needed. They will be automatically updated even when turned off. When an index is turned on (active), it will control the order in which the records are displayed; when turned off, indexes have no effect on the original database's display order.

Table 4-2 shows the MASTER file and its INDEX file. Note that the INDEX file is arranged alphabetically by name and that the MASTER file's record numbers remain unaffected by indexing. For example, the record for Brown retains the MASTER file's record number (2) in the INDEX file even though it will display first, while the record for Murphy is still record 1 even though it will display sixth.

WITH INDEX FILE ACTIVE			MASTER FILE		
Index/ display order	Name	Master file record number	MASTER record number	Name	City/State
1	BROWN	2	1	MURPHY	LEE, IL
2	HENDERSON	6	2	BROWN	MAR, CA
3	JONES	3	3	JONES	LEE, IL
4	MCCLURE	4	4	MCCLURE	LEE, IL
5	MOLANDER	7	5	ODEGARD	OAK, CA
6	MURPHY	1	6	HENDERSON	NEWARK, NJ
7	ODEGARD	5	7	MOLANDER	SEATTLE, WA

Table 4-2: The Indexed MASTER File

Indexing on the Database Design Screen

You can use either the Edit/Browse screen or the Database design screen to create an index. In the current exercise, you will use the Database design screen to create an index file on the customer name. Later, you will use the Edit/Browse screen to create an index for zip code and customer name.

To index on the customer name field, place the highlight on top of MASTER and,

1. Press **[Enter]**.
2. Type **M** to select **Modify structure/order**.
3. Press **[Esc]** to close the Organize menu.
4. Use the down arrow **[↓]** to move down to the CUST_NAME field.
5. Press **[Enter]** or **[Tab]** three times to move to the Index column.
6. Type **Y** on top of the N to instruct dBASE to create an index on the CUST_NAME field for you (as shown in Figure 4-7).
7. Press **[Alt]-[E]** to open the Exit menu.
8. Type **S** to select Save changes and exit.

Several messages appear, including INDEX ON CUST_NAME
TAG CUST_NAME. That means dBASE is indexing based upon
the entries in the CUST_NAME field, and the name (tag) for this
index is CUST_NAME. When you use the design screen to create
an index, the tag will always be the field name.

You are returned to the Control Center.

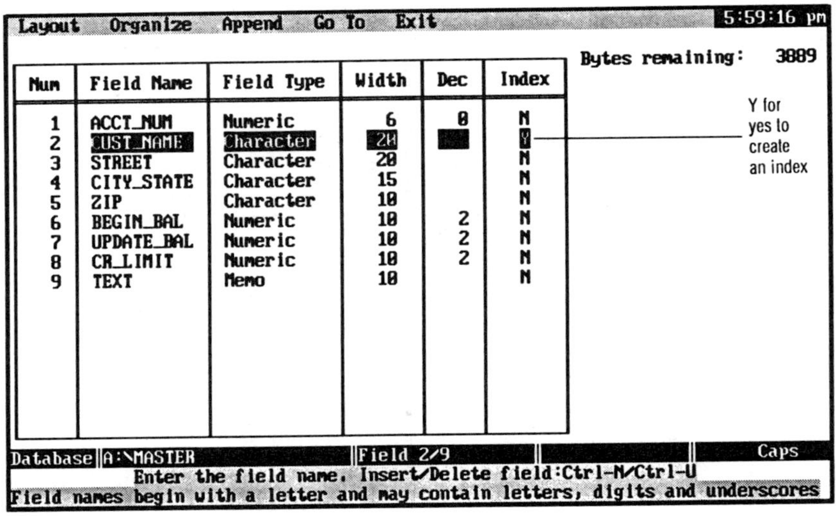

Figure 4-7:
*Indexing on
the Database
Design
Screen*

A newly created index is immediately in effect. However, when the
database is closed the index is closed, and when the database is
opened again, the index is **not** automatically opened--you must inten-
tionally open it. Thus, this time only, you do not need to open the
index; it is active.

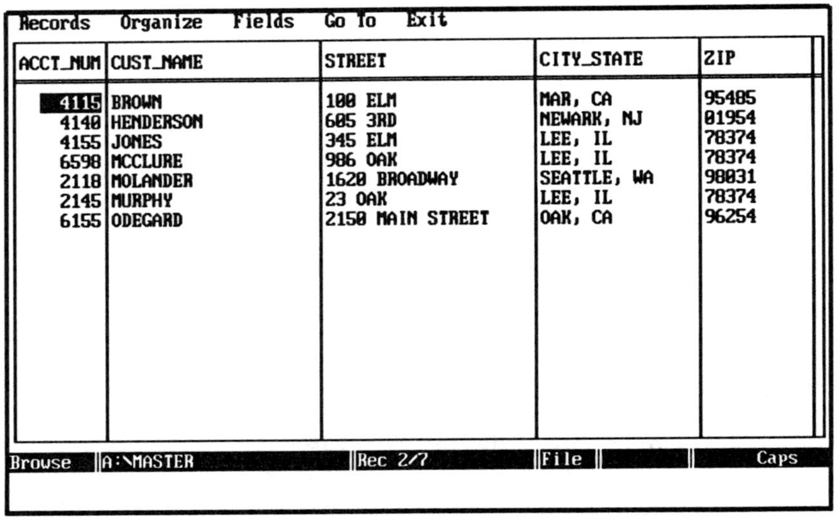

Figure 4-8:
*The File
Indexed by
Customer
Name*

To view the data in indexed order,

1.   View MASTER in Browse mode.
2.   Use the Go To menu to jump to the top of the database.
         Notice that the names are in order (as shown in Figure 4-8).
3.   Press the down arrow [↓] repeatedly while watching the record numbers in the Status Bar.
         The index is forcing the display into alphabetical order, not record number order.

Creating an Index in Browse Mode

While the Database design screen can create indexes for single fields only, the Organize menu in Edit or Browse mode can create compound indexes as well as single indexes.

You will index MASTER by ZIP and CUST_NAME, simultaneously. You sorted by the same pair of fields, but the sort order had to apply to a separate database. An index applies to the original database, meaning only one database needs to be maintained, yet it can be ordered with indexes in many different ways.

Since you are already on the Browse screen, to index MASTER by ZIP and CUST_NAME,

1.   Open the Organize menu.
2.   Select **Create new index**.
         The Index pop-up menu appears (as shown in Figure 4-9).

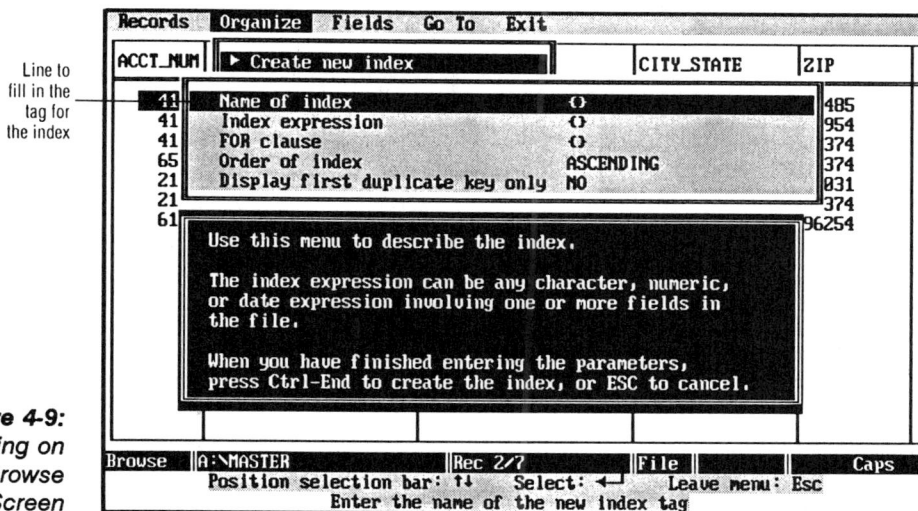

Figure 4-9: Indexing on the Browse Screen

3.   Type **N** to enter the tag (Name) for this index.
4.   Enter the name **ZIPANDNAME** and press **[Enter]**.
         The rules for naming indexes are the same as for naming fields.
5.   Type **I** to enter the Index expression.

6.   Enter **ZIP+CUST_NAME** and press **[Enter]** (as shown in Figure 4-10).

The plus sign means that within the index the second field should be tacked onto the end of the first field, making a combination of the two.

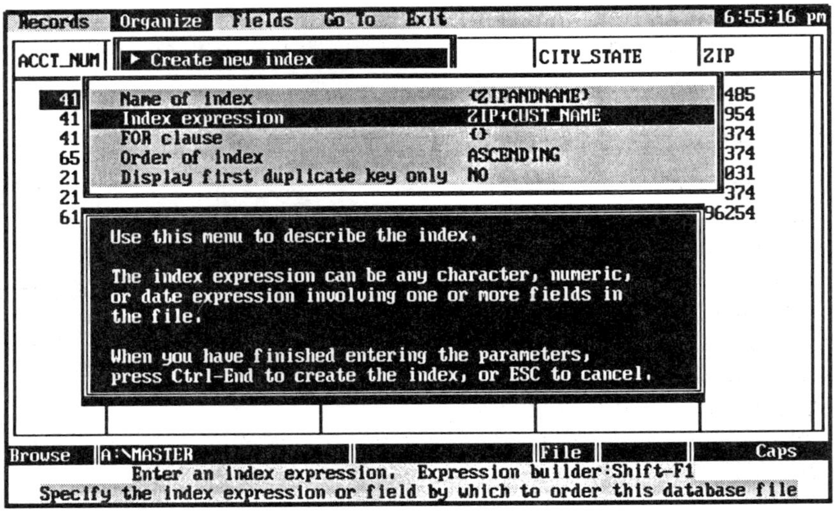

Figure 4-10:
Filling in the
Index Box

7.   Press **[Ctrl]-[End]** since you do not want to change the remaining three items.

After some messages, the order of the records on the Browse screen changes. The records are now in ZIP code combined with CUST_NAME order.

There are now two indexes available on MASTER. ZIPANDNAME is currently controlling the display. The CUST_NAME single index has been automatically closed, but can be reopened later.

Field	Data
Account Number	3456
Name	DONOVAN
Street	987 MAGIC MILE
City	NEWPORT, OR
Zip	97123
Beginning balance	100.00
Updated balance	100.00
Credit Limit	500.00

Table 4-3: Additional data for the MASTER file

To illustrate the dynamic quality of indexing, in the following exercise you will add another record to the file. You are still in Browse mode.

1. Use the Go To menu to move to the last record.
2. Press the down arrow [↓] and dBASE IV will ask "Add new records? (Y/N)."
3. Type **Y** to move onto a new line.
4. Add the information in Table 4-3 to the MASTER file, leaving the TEXT field empty.

Both index files will be automatically updated and the display ordered as soon as you Exit.

1. Open the Exit menu and pick Exit to save the new record. You are returned to the Control Center. To see where the new record is listed,
2. Display the data in Browse mode again. The record for Donovan retains the number 8, but is listed by ZIP code between Odegard and Molander, as shown in Figure 4-11. (If necessary, use the Go To menu to move to the top of the database.)

```
  Records   Organize   Fields   Go To   Exit

 ACCT_NUM│CUST_NAME           │STREET           │CITY_STATE    │ZIP

    4140 │HENDERSON           │605 3RD          │NEWARK, NJ    │01954
    4155 │JONES               │345 ELM          │LEE, IL       │78374
    6590 │MCCLURE             │986 OAK          │LEE, IL       │78374
    2145 │MURPHY              │23 OAK           │LEE, IL       │78374
    4115 │BROWN               │100 ELM          │MAR, CA       │95405
    6155 │ODEGARD             │2150 MAIN STREET │OAK, CA       │96254
    3456 │DONOVAN             │987 MAGIC MILE   │NEWPORT, OR   │97123
    2110 │MOLANDER            │1620 BROADWAY    │SEATTLE, WA   │98031




 Browse  ║A:\MASTER         ║        ║Rec 8/8    ║    ║File║    ║        Caps
```

Figure 4-11:
The Indexed
Data

Switching Indexes

To see how to switch to another existing index, and also to demonstrate that all indexes are automatically updated when the data are changed, you will change to the CUST_NAME index. As you are still in Browse mode,

1. Open the Organize menu.
2. Type the letter **O** to select Order records by index. A pop-up menu lists all available indexes for MASTER, as well as "Natural Order." Natural Order means the original order in which the data were entered, that is, with no index controlling the display order. That choice disengages any index.

3.   Move the highlight bar on top of **CUST_NAME**.
       Notice that a pop-up window shows the combination of fields
       used to create the index.
4.   Press **[Enter]**.
       You will see the message SET ORDER TO TAG CUST_NAME as
       the index is activated. The names should now be in alphabetical
       order, including the new name.

   You have now completed all of the exercises in Lesson 4. At this
point, you can continue or quit. If you decide to quit, remember to exit
properly, because failure to exit before you turn the computer off can
result in loss of data!

Review Exercises

1.   List the steps necessary to sort your name and address file
       (PRAC1) on the name field.
2.   List the steps necessary to sort your name and address file on
       the name field and the state field.
3.   List the steps necessary to create an index that will keep your
       name and address file in alphabetical order by the person's
       name.
4.   Using your PRAC1 name and address file, perform the following
       tasks:
       A. Sort the file by city to a database named PRACSORT. Exam-
           ine the new file, then switch back to PRAC1.
       B. Create an index that will keep PRAC1 in alphabetical order
           by name.
       C. Display all of the records in the file.
       D. Create another index that will keep the name and address
           file in order by state.
       E. Add one new record to the name and address file.
       F. Display the entire file.
       G. Create a query to display only the name and state fields for
           all of the records in the file.

5
Update Queries

The objectives of this lesson are to
- ▶ Delete records with a query
- ▶ Remove a file from the catalog
- ▶ Update records in a query
- ▶ Use the condition box

The Delete Query

In Chapter 2 you deleted records one at a time. Sometimes you may have large numbers of records to delete at one time. For example, once a year you might delete all bad credit risks from the MASTER file. You can use a delete query to mark for deletion all records that meet a specific condition. For example, to mark for deletion the records for all customers in RECSORT2 with an updated balance lower than 500.00,

1. Open RECSORT2. (Move the highlight bar on top of the name and press **[Enter]**, and then select Use file.)
2. Move the highlight bar on top of <create> in the Queries panel, and press **[Enter]**.
3. Press **[Alt]-[U]** to open the Update menu.
4. Type **S** to pick Select update operation (as shown in Figure 5-1).
5. Type **M** to select Mark records for deletion.
6. Press **P** to pick Proceed when the message "Changing this view query to an update query will delete the view skeleton" appears (as shown in Figure 5-2).

dBASE IV fills in the word "Mark" below the table name and removes the view skeleton. Since you are asking dBASE IV to operate on the data by marking records for deletion, and not to see the result of a search for matching records, you do not need the view skeleton. The word Mark is a code word telling dBASE that this query will mark records for deletion.

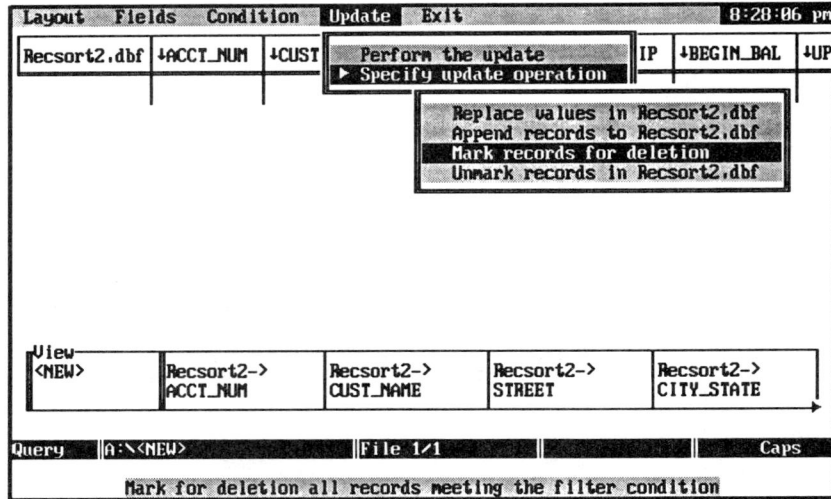

Figure 5-1:
*Selecting an
Update
Query*

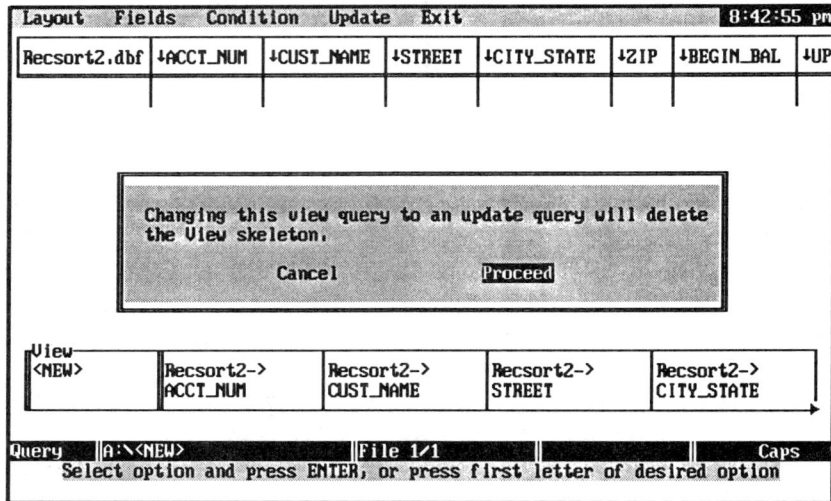

Figure 5-2:
*Removing
the View
Skeleton*

Since you want to delete all records with an updated balance below
$500,

7.   Press **[Tab]** several times to move to the UPDATE_BAL field.
8.   Type **<500** to fill in the criterion and press **[Enter]** (as shown in
     Figure 5-3).
9.   Press **[Alt]-[U]** to open the Update menu.
10. Type **P** to pick Perform the update.
     To answer the pop-up box asking "5 records will be marked for
     deletion -- OK?",
11. Type **Y** to answer Yes.

```
Layout  Fields  Condition  Update  Exit                    8:41:26 pm
┌Target────
│Recsort2.dbf│ CITY_STATE │ ZIP │ BEGIN_BAL │ UPDATE_BAL │ CR_LIMIT │ TEXT │
                                              ◄
 Mark        │            │     │           │ <500       │          │      │




Query   A:\<NEW>                  Field 7/9                       Caps
        Prev/Next field:Shift-Tab/Tab  Data:F2  Size:Shift-F7  Prev/Next skel:F3/F4
```

Figure 5-3:
The Filled-in Skeleton

The message "5 records deleted" is displayed. Another pop-up box (as shown in Figure 5-4) appears saying "Press any key to continue" and hinting that the **[F2]** key will display the changed data. To continue,

12.　　Press **[Enter]**.

```
Layout  Fields  Condition  Update  Exit                    8:44:25 pm
┌Target────
│Recsort2.dbf│ CITY_STATE │ ZIP │ BEGIN_BAL │ UPDATE_BAL │ CR_LIMIT │ TEXT │
 Mark        │
              ┌──────────────────────────────────┐
              │  Press F2 on Query Design Screen to │
              │  see changes                        │
              │                                     │
              │     Press any key to continue...    │
              └──────────────────────────────────┘
       ┌───────────────────────────────────────────┐
       │        5 records will be marked for deletion - OK? Y
       │ RECSORT2: Record No      1
       │        5 records deleted
       └───────────────────────────────────────────┘

Query   A:\<NEW>                  Field 7/9                       Caps
```

Figure 5-4:
The Delete Query Messages

To verify that five records were marked,

1.　　Press **[F2]** to view the data.
2.　　Press **[F2]** to switch to the Browse screen, if necessary.
3.　　Use the Go To menu to move to the Top record.

4.   Press **[Tab]** several times to move into the UPDATE_BAL field. Watching the last section of the Status Bar for the Del that marks a deleted record,

5.   Press the down arrow **[↓]** to visit each record.
      Notice that each time the updated balance is less than $500, the record is marked with the Del marker.

As previously mentioned, a database file may eventually contain many deleted records. You could allow the marked records to remain in the database, unmark them ("Unmark all records" in the Organize menu), or erase the marked records. You will erase them. To remove these records physically from the database file,

1.   Type **[Alt]-[O]** (the letter O) to open the Organize menu.

2.   Press **E** to select Erase marked records.
      In the resulting box,

3.   Type **Y** to answer Yes to "Are you sure you want to erase all marked records?" (as shown in Figure 5-5.)
      The messages "PACK" and "2 records copied" appear. PACK is the command that erases the records. Only two records remain, so only two were copied into the updated database.

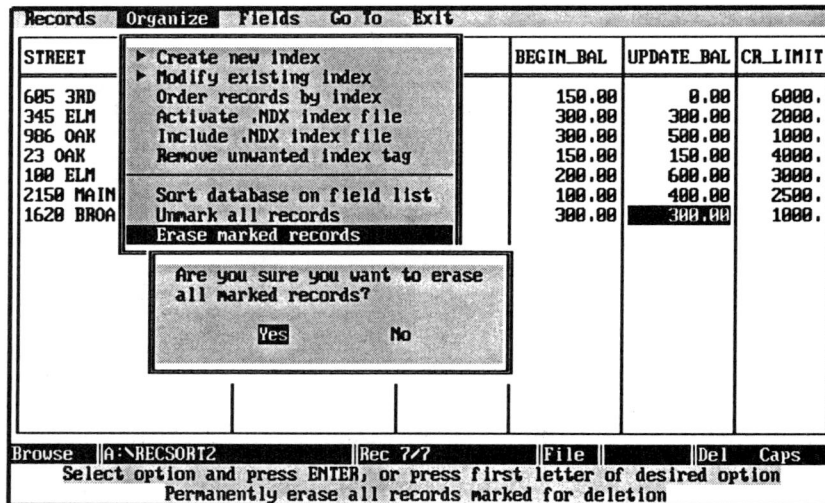

Figure 5-5:
Erasing the Marked Records

```
 Records  Organize  Fields  Go To  Exit
 ┌────────┬─────────────────────────────┬──────────┬──────────┬────────┐
 │STREET  │ ▶ Create new index          │BEGIN_BAL │UPDATE_BAL│CR_LIMIT│
 │        │ ▶ Modify existing index     │          │          │        │
 │605 3RD │   Order records by index    │   150.00 │     0.00 │  6000. │
 │345 ELM │   Activate .NDX index file  │   300.00 │   300.00 │  2000. │
 │986 OAK │   Include .NDX index file   │   300.00 │   500.00 │  1000. │
 │23 OAK  │   Remove unwanted index tag │   150.00 │   150.00 │  4000. │
 │100 ELM │                             │   200.00 │   600.00 │  3000. │
 │2150 MAIN   Sort database on field list│  100.00 │   400.00 │  2500. │
 │1620 BROA   Unmark all records        │   300.00 │   300.00 │  1000. │
 │        │   Erase marked records      │          │          │        │
 │        ├─────────────────────────────┤          │          │        │
 │        │ Are you sure you want to erase│        │          │        │
 │        │ all marked records?         │          │          │        │
 │        │      Yes        No          │          │          │        │
 │        └─────────────────────────────┘          │          │        │
 │                                                                     │
 │                                                                     │
 ├─────────────────────────────────────────────────────────────────┤
 │Browse ║A:\RECSORT2       ║Rec 7/7      ║File ║    ║Del   Caps      │
 │   Select option and press ENTER, or press first letter of desired option │
 │        Permanently erase all records marked for deletion           │
 └─────────────────────────────────────────────────────────────────┘
```

4.   Press **[Alt]-[E]** to open the Exit menu.

5.   Type **T** to pick Transfer to Query Design.
      You do not need to save the query. To abandon the query design,

6.   Type **[Alt]-[E]** to open the Exit menu.

7.   Press **A** to select Abandon changes and exit.

8.   Press **Y** to select Yes in the "Are you sure you want to abandon operation?" box.

9.   Display the data in RECSORT2 to confirm that only 2 records remain.

10.   Return to the Control Center.

Removing a File from the Catalog

Some database files will eventually outgrow their usefulness. Removing a file from the catalog will keep the task panels less cluttered and make selecting the proper files easier. When you remove a file from the catalog, dBASE IV also gives you the choice of erasing the file from the disk. RECSORT2 has served its purpose; to remove it from the catalog and erase it from the disk,

1.   Close the file. (An open file cannot be erased.)

2.   Move the highlight bar on top of RECSORT2.

3.   Type **[Alt]-[C]** to open the Catalog menu.

4.   Press **R** to select Remove highlighted file from catalog (as shown in Figure 5-6).

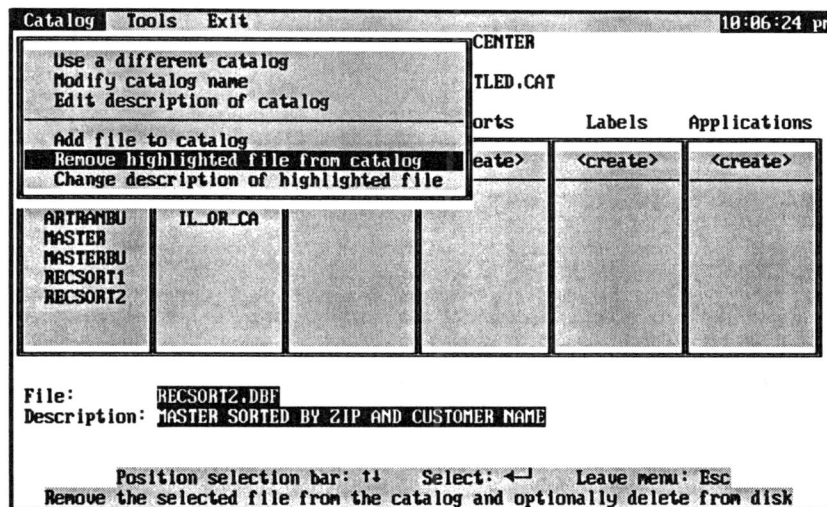

Figure 5-6: *Removing the File from the Catalog*

5.   Type **Y** to answer Yes to "Are you sure you want to remove this file from the catalog?"

6.   Also type **Y** to answer Yes to "Do you also want to delete this file from the disk?"

      The RECSORT2 file is no longer listed in the Data panel, and no longer exists.

The Replace Query

You can change or update the contents of the records in a file by using a Replace query. In the following exercise, you will change all of the MASTER file records in which a city name is misspelled. To change the name of LEE, IL to LEI, IL in the CITY_STATE field,

1. Highlight <create> in the Queries panel and press **[Enter]**.

Since no database file was open, the query screen is empty, and the Layout menu is automatically open with the highlight bar on Add file to query. To change the city name in MASTER, you must add the MASTER skeleton to the query screen. Not having any database open when you entered the query design screen suppressed the view skeleton.
To add the MASTER file skeleton,

2. Type **A** to pick Add file to query.
3. Move the highlight on top of MASTER.DBF in the list (as shown in Figure 5-7) and press **[Enter]**.
The file skeleton for MASTER appears, but no view skeleton.

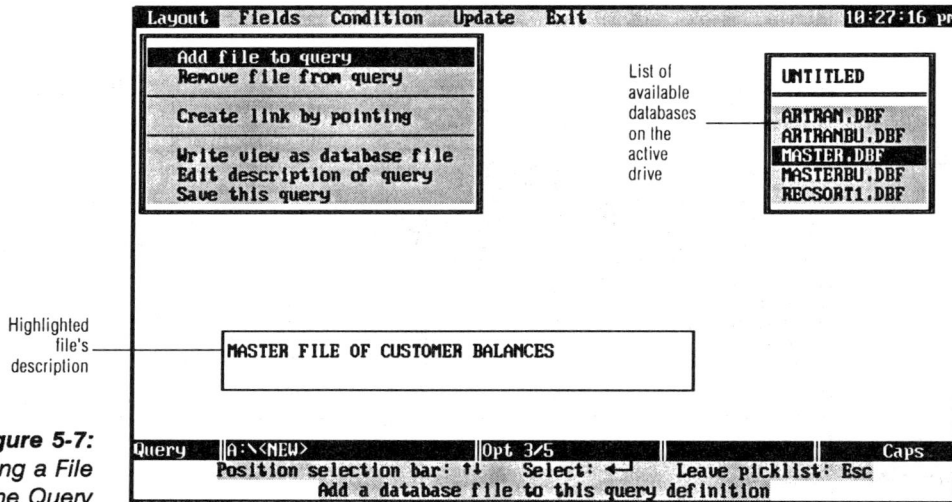

Figure 5-7:
Adding a File
to the Query

4. Press **[Alt]-[U]** to open the Update menu.
5. Type **S** to pick Select update operation.
6. Type **R** to select Replace values in Master.dbf (as shown in Figure 5-8).
dBASE IV enters the code word "Replace" under the table name.
7. Press **[Tab]** several times to move to the CITY_STATE field.
8. Type **="LEE, IL"** for the criterion to select the proper records to be changed.
You must enter the new value for the city/state in the very same field. To enter more than one item in a single field, separate the items with commas. Also, the new value must be preceded by the word **WITH**.

```
 Layout   Fields   Condition   Update   Exit                    10:30:06 pm
  Master.dbf      ACCT_NUM    CUST   Perform the update        IP   BEGIN_BAL   UP
                                   ▶ Specify update operation

                                    ┌─────────────────────────────────┐
                                    │ Replace values in Master.dbf     │
                                    │ Append records to Master.dbf     │
                                    │ Mark records for deletion        │
                                    │ Unmark records in Master.dbf     │
                                    └─────────────────────────────────┘




 Query    A:\<NEW>                     File 1/1                          Caps
 Replace field contents using "with" values, in records meeting query condition
```

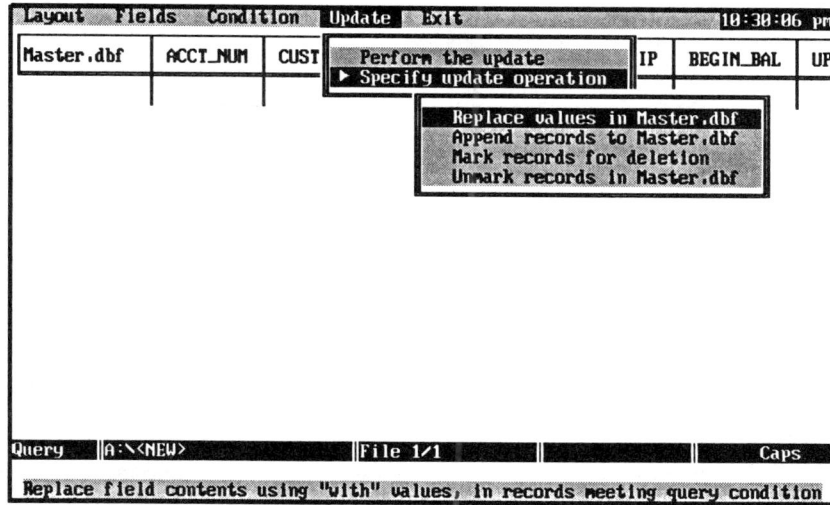

Figure 5-8: *Selecting the Replace Query*

To specify the separator and the new value,

9.   Type **,WITH "LEI, IL"** (as shown in Figure 5-9) and press **[Enter]**.

In an update query, the database becomes a target

```
 Layout   Fields   Condition   Update   Exit                    10:46:24 pm
 ─Target─
  Master.dbf      ACCT_NUM    CUST_NAME    STREET    CITY_STATE           ZIP

  Replace                                          ="LEE, IL",WITH "LEI, IL"


                                                      Separator
                                                      comma










 Query    A:\<NEW>                     Field 4/9                         Caps
 Prev/Next field:Shift-Tab/Tab   Data:F2   Size:Shift-F7   Prev/Next skel:F3/F4
```

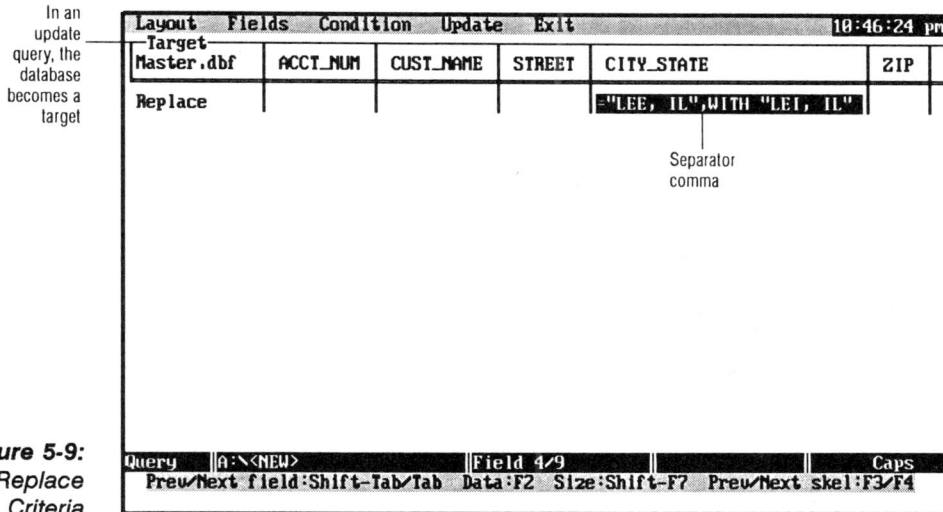

Figure 5-9: *The Replace Criteria*

To perform the change,

10.   Press **[Alt]-[U]** to open the Update menu.

11.   Type **P** to pick Perform the update.
        The message "3 records replaced" is displayed. Another pop-up box appears saying "Press any key to continue" and hinting that the **[F2]** key will display the changed data (as shown in Figure 5-10). As instructed,

12. Press **[Enter]**.

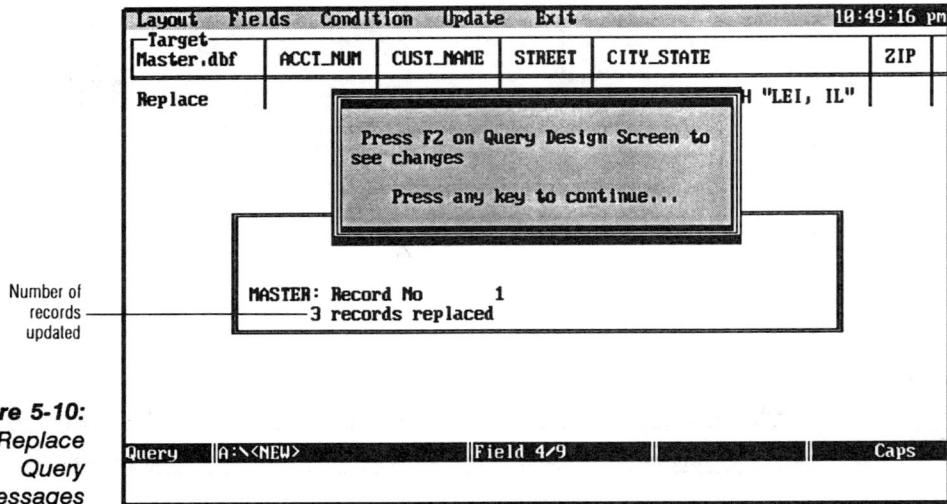

Figure 5-10:
The Replace Query Messages

Number of records updated

To verify that the three records were changed,

1. Press **[F2]** to view the data. (Switch to Browse, if necessary.)
2. Use the Go To menu to move to the Top record.
    Each occurrence of LEE, IL has been replaced with LEI, IL (as shown in Figure 5-11).

Figure 5-11:
The Changed Records

3. Press **[Alt]-[E]** to open the Exit menu.
4. Type **T** to pick Transfer to Query Design.
    You do not need to save this query. To abandon the query design,
5. Type **[Alt]-[E]** to open the Exit menu.

6.   Press **A** to select Abandon changes and exit.

7.   Press **Y** to select Yes in the "Are you sure you want to abandon operation?" box.

The Condition Box

In Chapter 3 you searched for matching data with a query. Examples searched for character, date, and numeric data. Memo fields can also be searched, but the criterion is not allowed in the file skeleton. The criterion must be placed in the Condition Box. A condition box is added to the query design screen by selecting from the Condition menu.

Many of the TEXT field entries in MASTER had the word "CREDIT" somewhere within them. To search the memo fields for that word,

1.   Open MASTER (so that the name is above the line in the Data panel, if necessary).

2.   Create a query.

3.   Press **[F5]** while under the table name to remove all fields from the view.

4.   Press **[Tab]** twice to move to CUST_NAME, and press **[F5]** to include it in the view.

5.   Press **[End]** to jump to TEXT (the end field), and press **[F5]** to include it in the view.

6.   Type **[Alt]-[C]** to open the Condition menu.

7.   Press **A** to select Add condition box (as shown in Figure 5-12). The condition box appears between the MASTER skeleton and the view skeleton, and the cursor is in the Condition box.

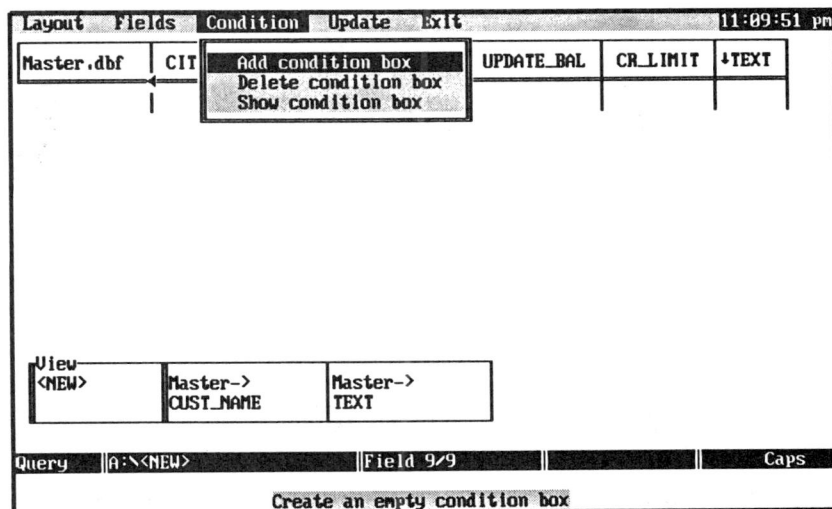

Figure 5-12: *Adding a Condition Box*

To specify the search criterion,

8.   Type **"CREDIT" $ TEXT** and press **[Enter]** (as shown in Figure 5-13).

Since the dollar sign means "is contained in," this criterion means the word CREDIT must be contained somewhere within the entry in the TEXT field.

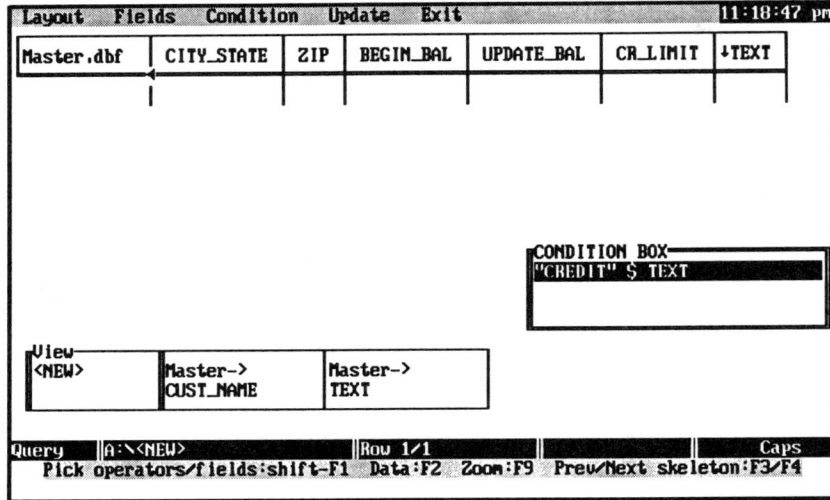

```
Layout  Fields  Condition  Update  Exit              11:18:47 pm
┌───────────┬───────────┬─────┬──────────┬────────────┬──────────┬───────┐
│Master.dbf │ CITY_STATE│ ZIP │ BEGIN_BAL│ UPDATE_BAL │ CR_LIMIT │↓TEXT  │
│           │     │          │          │            │          │       │
└───────────┴───────────┴─────┴──────────┴────────────┴──────────┴───────┘


                                              ┌CONDITION BOX────────┐
                                              │"CREDIT" $ TEXT      │
                                              │                     │
                                              └─────────────────────┘

 ┌View────────────────────────────────────────────┐
 │<NEW>      ┌Master->─────┐ ┌Master->─────┐       │
 │           │CUST_NAME    │ │TEXT         │       │
 │           └─────────────┘ └─────────────┘       │
 └─────────────────────────────────────────────────┘
 Query   ║A:\<NEW>          ║Row 1/1                        Caps
    Pick operators/fields:shift-F1  Data:F2  Zoom:F9  Prev/Next skeleton:F3/F4
```

Figure 5-13:
The Filled-in
Criterion

9. Press **[F2]** to examine the answer.
    Four records match the criterion. To confirm the contents,
10. Press **[Tab]** to move to the TEXT field.
11. Press **[F9]** to open the memo field and notice the word CREDIT.
    To close the memo field,
12. Press **[F9]**.
13. Move to each memo field and examine the contents with the **[F9]** key.

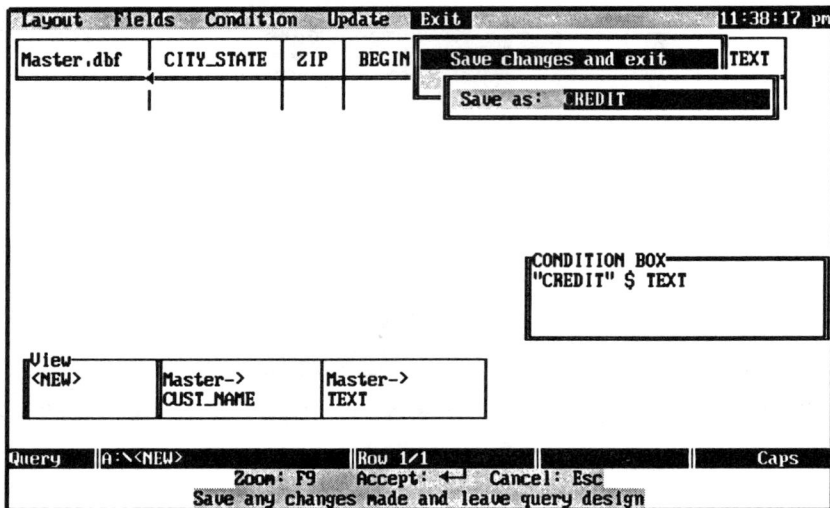

```
Layout  Fields  Condition  Update  Exit              11:38:17 pm
┌───────────┬───────────┬─────┬───────────────────────────────┬───────┐
│Master.dbf │ CITY_STATE│ ZIP │ BEGIN║ Save changes and exit  ║│TEXT   │
│           │     │          │      ╟────────────────────────╢│       │
│           │     │          │      ║ Save as:  CREDIT       ║│       │
└───────────┴───────────┴─────┴──────╚════════════════════════╝┴───────┘


                                              ┌CONDITION BOX────────┐
                                              │"CREDIT" $ TEXT      │
                                              │                     │
                                              └─────────────────────┘

 ┌View────────────────────────────────────────────┐
 │<NEW>      ┌Master->─────┐ ┌Master->─────┐       │
 │           │CUST_NAME    │ │TEXT         │       │
 │           └─────────────┘ └─────────────┘       │
 └─────────────────────────────────────────────────┘
 Query   ║A:\<NEW>          ║Row 1/1                        Caps
           Zoom: F9   Accept: ←┘  Cancel: Esc
           Save any changes made and leave query design
```

Figure 5-14:
Saving the
Query

14. Press **[Alt]-[E]** to open the Exit menu.

15.   Type **T** to pick Transfer to Query Design.
To save the query design,
16.   Type **[Alt]-[E]** to open the Exit menu.
17.   Press **S** to select Save changes and exit.
18.   Type the filename **CREDIT** in the Save as: box, and press **[Enter]** (as shown in Figure 5-14).
19.   Close CREDIT.

You have completed all of the exercises in Lesson 5. At this point, you can continue or quit. If you decide to quit, remember to properly exit from the program, because failure to close the files before turning the computer off can result in lost data!

Review Exercises

1.   List the steps necessary to delete records with a query.
2.   List the steps necessary to remove a file from the catalog.
3.   List the steps necessary to update data with a replace query.
4.   List the steps necessary to query a memo field using the condition box.
5.   Using your PRAC1 file,
    A. Use a delete query to mark for deletion all of the listings in New York.
    B. View the data and check for the Del marks.
    C. Remove the mark from one record.
    D. Use a replace query to replace Klovis with Clovis.
    E. View the data to confirm the changes.
    F. Pack the database file by selecting in the Organize menu Erase the marked records.
    G. Add a memo field named NOTES as a new last field in PRAC1.
    H. Fill in the memo fields; use the word MOVED in several of the notes.
    I. Query PRAC1 using the Condition box for those memos with the word MOVED in the note.

6

Printing Reports and Labels

The objectives of this lesson are to
- Create a custom report format
- Print a report
- Create a custom label format
- Print labels
- Observe the relationship between databases and report or label designs

Creating Reports

To this point, you have only been able to display your data on the screen. Now, you will use the Report function of dBASE IV to create reports that are more presentable and better reflect the data.

The Report function gives you the capability to print fields where you want them, and also to perform calculations on those fields. In any report, you can group together related data. Reports allow you to retrieve and manipulate your database information according to your own special needs.

dBASE IV has three basic report designs available: column, form, and mailmerge. A column design prints all included data in neat columns, one record after another, like the Browse screen. A form design allows you to place the data anywhere on the page as a free form report, like the Edit screen. A Mailmerge design will be mostly a form letter, with a few fields of data placed within the text.

For each of the designs, dBASE initially divides the report design screen into five sections or "bands." You place the data fields and labels that you want printed in each section of the report in the matching design band. The bands are described in Table 6-1.

In the following exercise, you will create a report based on ARTRAN. After you have created, displayed, and saved the report, you will print it.

NOTE: To create a report form, you must have a database file or query in use.

Band	Example
Page Header	Heading at top of every page
Report Intro	Title once only at beginning of report
Detail	Columns of data
Report Summary	Grand totals and final comments
Page Footer	Page number at bottom of each page

Table 6-1: Report Design Screen Bands

Creating a Report Format

To create a report format for the ARTRAN file,

1. Open ARTRAN for use so that it is above the horizontal line.
2. Move the highlight bar on top of <create> in the Reports panel (as shown in Figure 6-1) and press **[Enter]**.

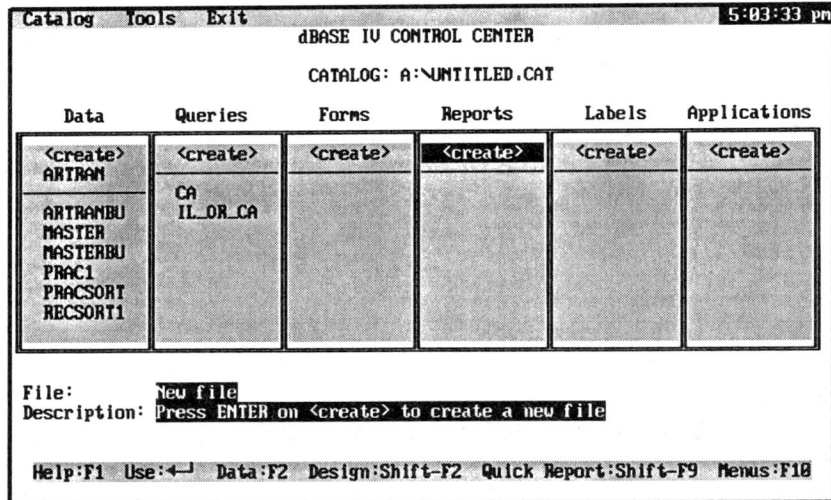

Figure 6-1:
Creating a
Report for
ARTRAN

An empty report design screen appears with the Layout menu open. Though you can close the menu and place each item on the design one by one, it is usually much quicker to utilize a "Quick layout." Selecting quick layout in the menu instructs dBASE IV to begin the design for you by placing every field on the screen and creating labels to name the columns of data. You may then modify the quick layout to create a custom design.

To create a Quick layout,

3. Press **Q** to pick Quick layout.
4. Type **C** to select Column layout (as shown in Figure 6-2).

A column design is created, as shown in Figure 6-3.

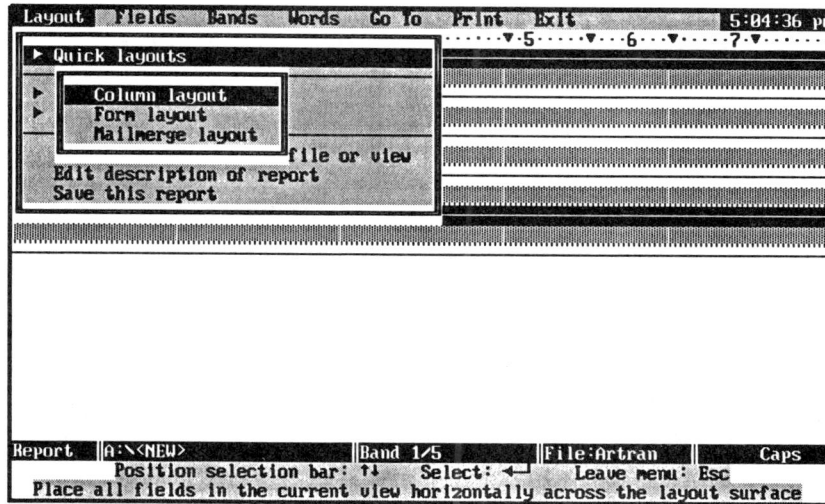

Figure 6-2:
Selecting a
Quick Layout

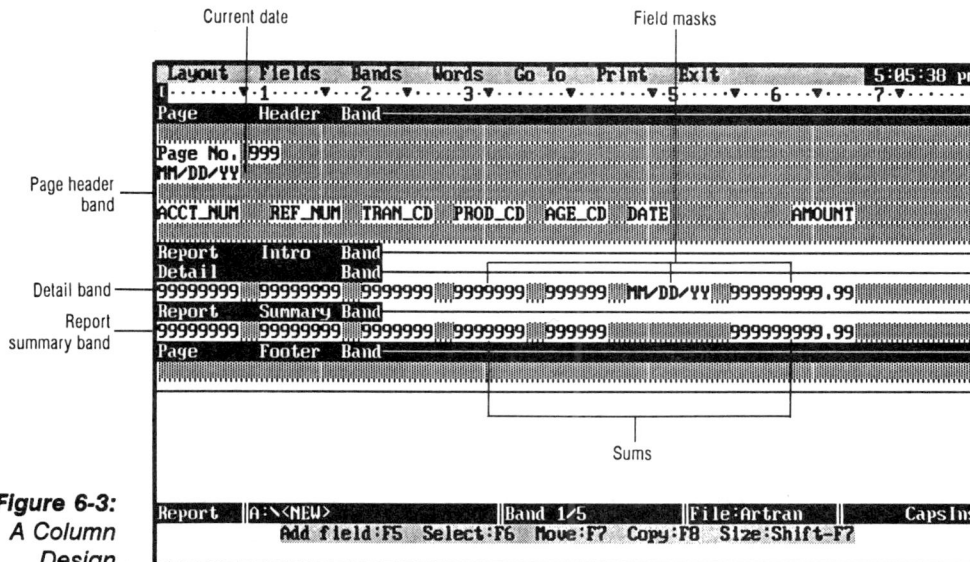

Current date   Field masks

Page header
band

Detail band

Report
summary band

Sums

Figure 6-3:
A Column
Design

Each field in ARTRAN is positioned side by side across the design screen, and the database's field names (ACCT_NUM, REF_NUM, etc.) are used as the headings at the tops of each column. In the actual report, the columns of data listings from the database file will be placed in the positions of the 9's and MM/DD/YY (the field "masks"), with each record immediately below the previous one. Thus, the Detail Band shows only the position of the first line of data.

A page number and the current date are included in the Page Header at the left margin. Each numerical field is given a grand total at the bottom of the column in the Report Summary Band. The Page Footer Band is currently empty, and the Report Intro Band is closed.

To see how the report mirrors the current design by previewing it on the screen,

5.   Press **[Alt]-[P]** to open the Print menu.

6.   Type **V** to select View report on screen.

Several messages will appear on the bottom screen lines as dBASE generates the report design. The generation could take several seconds.

Note: In order to create either reports or labels, or view them on the screen, the dBASE IV directory must be in the Disk Operating System's path. If you do not know how to check the current path, or how to add the dBASE IV directory to the path should it be missing, consult your Lab Coordinator. If dBASE IV is not in the path, you will get a "Cannot open dbase3.res resource file" error, and you will not be able to create the report.

Page No.	1					
08/02/92						
ACCT_NUM	REF_NUM	TRAN_CD	PROD_CD	AGE_CD	DATE	AMOUNT
6598	11458	4	0	1	01/17/88	-75.00
6155	11459	4	0	1	01/17/88	-13.50
2145	77145	1	45	0	01/17/88	50.00
4155	77146	1	39	0	01/17/88	10.00
19053	177208	10	84	2		-28.50

Row of sums ──

Cancel viewing: ESC, Continue viewing: SPACEBAR

Figure 6-4:
Viewing the Report on the Screen

The preview (as shown in Figure 6-4) shows the seven columns of data, as well as the six grand totals at the bottoms of the numerical columns. While it does not make any sense to total the account numbers, dBASE always includes totals for all numerical fields in a quick layout.

To return to the design screen,

7.   Press the **[spacebar]** three times (as suggested in the message line).

Refining the Report Design

You can make several improvements to this report design. The totals for ACCT_NUM and REF_NUM make no sense and should be removed. Lines should be added between the last line of data and the remaining totals. A report heading could be typed in the Report Intro Band.

To remove the unneeded sums,

1.   Press the down arrow [↓] several times until the cursor is on top of the first 99999999 in the Report Summary Band. (The message line indicates what field the cursor is on; it should say "Operation: SUM Summarize: ACCT_NUM.")
2.   Press **[Alt]-[F]** to open the Fields menu.
3.   Type **R** to select Remove field.
      The field mask will disappear.
      To remove the sum of the REF_NUM column,
4.   Press the right arrow [→] several times until the cursor is on top of its field mask and the message line says "Operation: SUM Summarize: REF_NUM."
5.   Press **[Alt]-[F]** to open the Fields menu.
6.   Type **R** to select Remove field.
      The field mask will disappear. To jump to the left margin,
7.   Press **[Home]**.
      Note at the right end of the Status Bar that insert is on, then,
8.   Press **[Enter]** to insert a blank line above the remaining sums.
9.   Press the up arrow [↑] to move onto the new blank line.
      To draw the line above the sum,
10.   Press the right arrow [→] several times to move above the first 9 of the TRAN_CD field.
11.   Type **[Alt]-[L]** to open the Layout menu.
12.   Press **L** to select Line.
13.   Type **S** to pick Single.
14.   Press **[Enter]** to indicate that the cursor is at the beginning position for the line as instructed on the message line.
15.   Press the right arrow [→] seven times to draw the line.
16.   Press **[Enter]** to complete the line, as instructed in the message line.
17.   Repeat steps 10 through 16 to draw lines above each sum (as shown in Figure 6-5).

Note: Not all printers are capable of printing the line characters. They would substitute other letters in place of the lines.

To prepare for a centered report title,
1.   Press **[Home]** to jump to the left margin.
2.   Press the up arrow [↑] until the cursor is on top of the line that says Report Intro Band.
3.   Press **[Enter]** to open this band.

4. Press the down arrow [↓] to move onto the new line of the Report Intro Band.
5. Press **[Enter]** twice to insert two more blank lines in this band.
6. Press the up arrow [↑] once to move onto the middle line of the three.

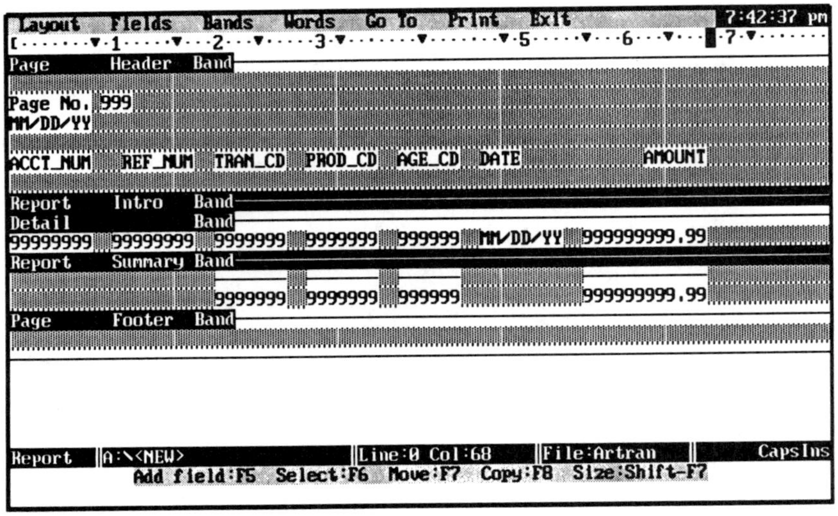

Figure 6-5: *Drawing the Lines Above the Sums*

dBASE IV has made the report width 254 characters wide. The left margin begins at the open square bracket on the left end of the ruler on the second screen line. The right square bracket is far off the right side of the screen at 254. Your report will only be 80 characters wide, so you need to adjust the right margin. This will also assure that the title is properly centered. To adjust the right margin,

1. Press **[Alt]-[W]** to open the Words menu.
2. Type **M** to select Modify ruler.
    The cursor will jump onto the ruler at the top of the screen. The ruler is marked off with digits that represent each ten spaces and downward pointing triangles that mark the tab stops.
3. Press the **[Tab]** key several times to get near 78 on the ruler, then press left or right arrow keys until the cursor is at 78.
4. Type] to fix the right margin.
    A square bracket will appear at 78 on the ruler, as shown in Figure 6-6.
5. Press **[Enter]** to complete the operation.

To enter and center the title,

1. Type **ACCOUNTS RECEIVABLE TRANSACTIONS** for the report title.
    To select the title so that you can center it,

2. Press **[F6]** (as indicated in the navigation line).
3. Press **[Home]** to jump to the left margin.
4. Press **[Enter]** to complete the selection.
   The title is highlighted, indicating that it is the currently selected item.
5. Type **[Alt]-[W]** to open the Words menu.
6. Press **P** to select Position.
7. Type **C** to pick Center.
8. Press **[Esc]** just once to remove the selection.

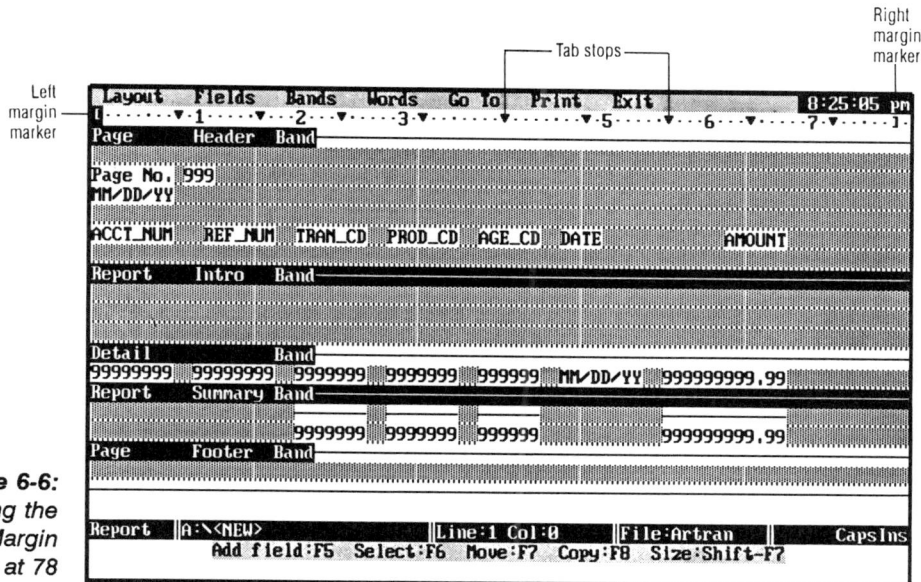

Figure 6-6: Setting the Right Margin Position at 78

Note: If you accidentally press the [Esc] key too many times, dBASE IV will think you wish to abort the current design and ask "Are you sure you want to abandon operation?" Be sure to always answer N for No, unless you really do want to abort the design.

Note: When you have selected anything on a design screen, be careful not to press the [Del] (or [Delete]) key, for that key would delete the selection. Also, be sure to remove the selection with the [Esc] key as soon as you are finished with it.

The Report Intro Band is currently below the Page Header Band. That means that the report header would appear below the column headings in the page header. To reverse the positions of the page header and report header,

1. Press **[Alt]-[B]** to open the Bands menu.
2. Type **P** to select Page heading in report intro.
   The YES in the menu will switch to NO, and the Page Header Band and Report Intro Band will trade places (as shown in Figure 6-7).

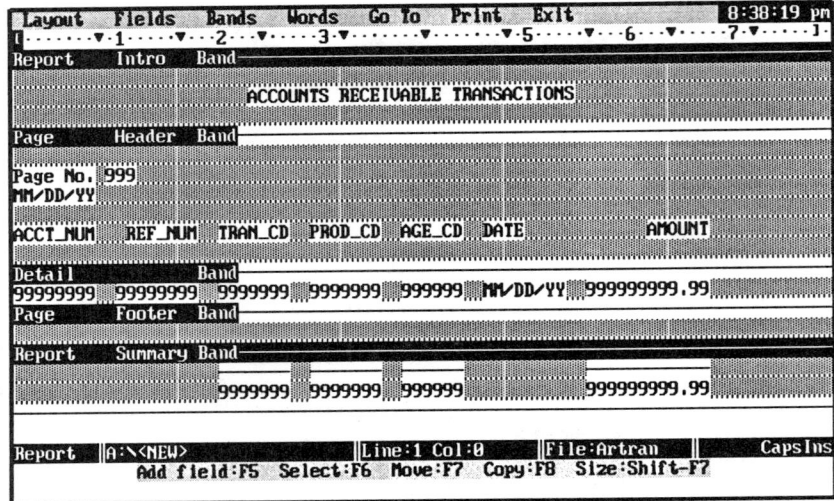

Figure 6-7:
Switching the Report Intro Band above the Page Header Band

This completes the first report design.

Thus, to preview and then save the report,

1. Press **[Alt]-[P]** to open the Print menu.
2. Type **V** to select View report on screen.
    The report should resemble Figure 6-8.

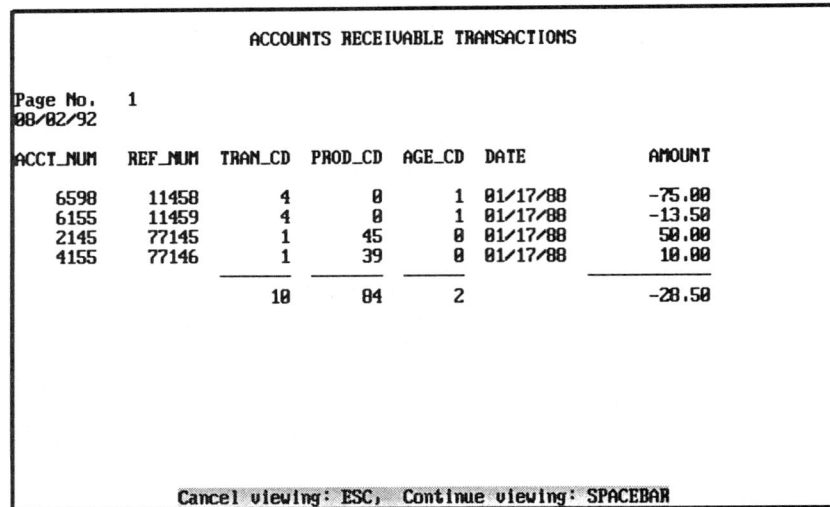

Figure 6-8:
The Completed Column Report

3. Press the **[spacebar]** three times to return to the design screen.
4. Press **[Alt]-[E]** to open the Exit menu.
5. Type **S** to select Save changes and exit.
6. Type the name **ARREPORT** and press **[Enter]**.

After dBASE generates the report design, you will be returned to the Control Center.

Printing the Report

To print the report,

1. Press **[Enter]** with the highlight bar on top of ARREPORT in the Reports panel.
2. Type **P** to select Print report.
    In the resulting pop-up menu (as shown in Figure 6-9),
3. Press **B** to Begin printing.

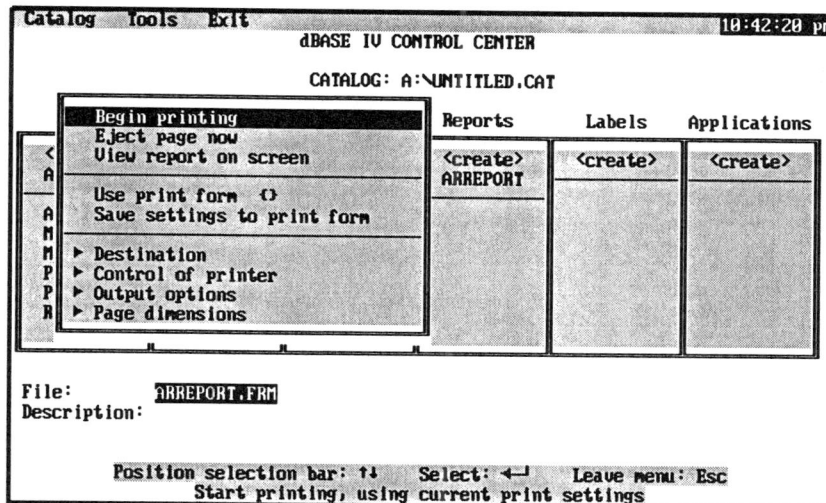

Figure 6-9:
The Print
Menu

Designing a Free Form Report from a Query

To restrict the data listings that are to be included in a report, you can design a report for a view (from a query). You will create a free form report for the IL_OR_CA view. To begin,

1. Open (use) the view.
    IL_OR_CA will move above the line in the Queries panel. (Any open database is closed.)
2. Press **[Enter]** with the highlight on <create> in the Reports panel.
3. Press **Q** to pick Quick layout.
4. Type **F** to select Form layout.
    A form design is created, as shown in Figure 6-10.
    To remove the unwanted fields,
5. Press the down arrow **[↓]** several times to move the cursor on top of the Z of ZIP.

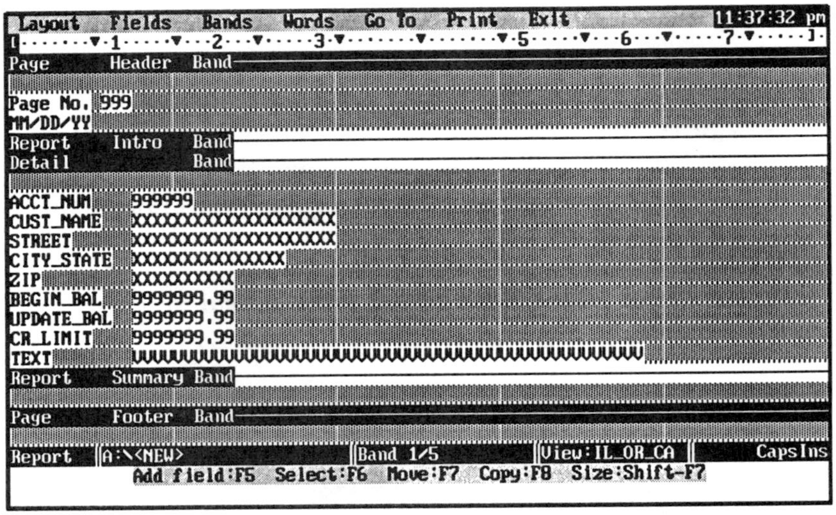

Figure 6-10:
A Form Design

6. Press **[Alt]-[W]** to open the Words menu.
7. Type **R** to select Remove line.
   The ZIP line disappears, and the lower lines move up.
8. Repeat steps 6 and 7 to remove BEGIN_BAL, UPDATE_BAL, and CR_LIMIT.
   To draw a line that will separate each record from the next,
9. Press the **[End]** key on the T of TEXT to jump to the end of the TEXT field.
10. Press **[Enter]** twice to insert two blank lines below TEXT.
11. Press **[Alt]-[L]** to open the Layout menu.
12. Type **L** to select Line.
13. Type **S** to pick Single.

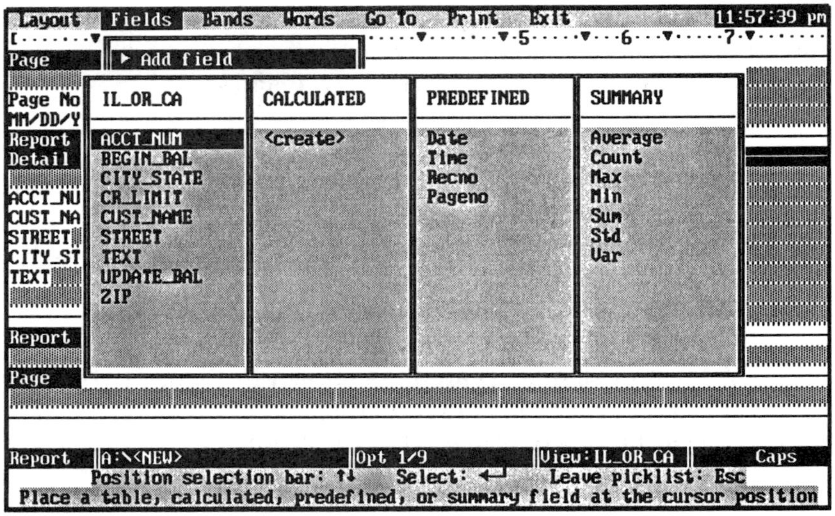

Figure 6-11:
Using the Picklist

14. Press **[Enter]** to start the line, press the right arrow **[→]** many times to draw the line to about 70 on the ruler (watch the highlight move on the ruler), and press **[Enter]** to complete the line.

To add the ZIP field at the end of the line with CITY_STATE,

15. Press **[Home]** to jump to the left margin.

16. Press the up arrow **[↑]** three times to move the cursor on top of the C of CITY_STATE.

17. Press **[End]** to jump to the end of the CITY_STATE field, and press the right arrow **[→]** to move to the right one more space.

18. Type **[Alt]-[F]** to open the Fields menu.

19. Press **A** to select Add field.

The picklist appears, as shown in Figure 6-11.

20. Move the highlight in the first column down onto ZIP, and press **[Enter]**.

The "Field Definition" menu appears (as shown in Figure 6-12). You do not want to change anything in it.

Figure 6-12:
The Field Definition Menu

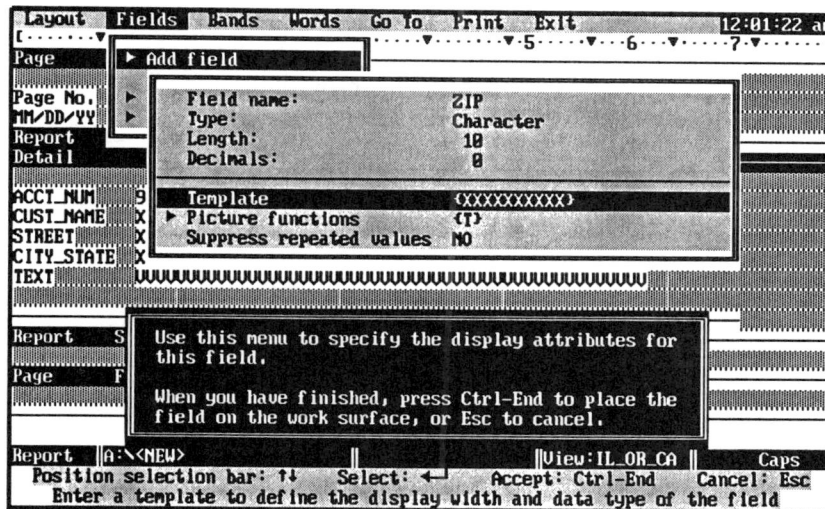

```
 Layout   Fields   Bands   Words   Go To   Print   Exit            12:01:22 am
[ · · · · · · ▼                      · · · · · ▼· · · · ▼· 5· · · · ▼· 6 · · ▼· · · · 7·▼· · · · · · · ·
 Page         ▶ Add field
 Page No.  ▶      Field name:            ZIP
 MM/DD/YY  ▶      Type:                  Character
 Report           Length:                10
 Detail           Decimals:              0

 ACCT_NUM  9      Template               {XXXXXXXXXX}
 CUST_NAME X    ▶ Picture functions      {I}
 STREET    X      Suppress repeated values  NO
 CITY_STATE X
 TEXT
              Use this menu to specify the display attributes for
 Report   S   this field.
 Page     F   When you have finished, press Ctrl-End to place the
              field on the work surface, or Esc to cancel.

 Report   A:\<NEW>                              View:IL_OR_CA         Caps
 Position selection bar: ↑↓     Select: ◀┘     Accept: Ctrl-End   Cancel: Esc
        Enter a template to define the display width and data type of the field
```

To accept the settings,

21. Press **[Ctrl]-[End]**.

The ZIP field appears near the end of the CITY_STATE field.

To preview the report,

22. Press **[Alt]-[P]** to open the Print menu.

23. Type **V** to select View report on screen.

24. Press the **[spacebar]** several times to return to the design screen.

Placing a Calculated Field on the Report

The credit remaining can be calculated by subtracting the UPDATE_BAL from the CR_LIMIT. Although that result is not in the database, it can be calculated on the report.

The cursor position within the current band is displayed in the third section of the Status Bar. To place the calculated field at Line:1 Col:40 in the Detail Band,

1. Press the up arrow [↑] three times to move the cursor onto Line:1.
2. Press the right arrow [→] two times to move the cursor to Col-:40.
3. Type the label **REMAINING BALANCE**, and press the **[spacebar]**.
4. Press **[Alt]-[F]** to open the Fields menu.
5. Type **A** to select Add field.
6. Press the right arrow [→] to move the cursor onto <create> in the CALCULATED column, and press **[Enter]**.
7. Type **N** to activate the Name line, and then type **REMAINING** and press **[Enter]**.
8. Type **E** to open the Expression line.
9. Press **[Shift]-[F1]** to open the picklist.
10. Move the highlight bar onto CR_LIMIT and press **[Enter]**.
11. Type a minus sign [-].
12. Press **[Shift]-[F1]** to open the picklist.
13. Move the highlight bar onto UPDATE_BAL and press **[Enter]**.
14. Press **[Enter]** to complete the expression (see Figure 6-13).

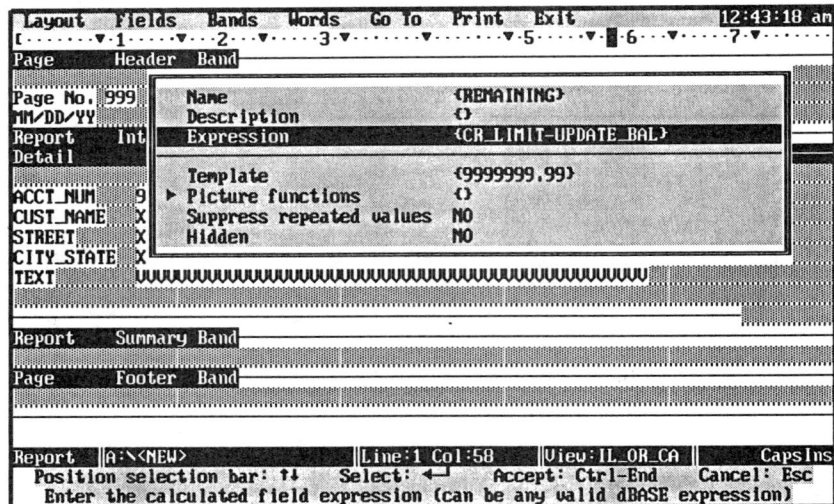

Figure 6-13: Entering the Expression

15. Press **[Ctrl]-[End]** to accept the field definition menu.
    The calculated field is placed on the design (as shown in Figure 6-14).
    To preview the report,
16. Press **[Alt]-[P]** to open the Print menu.
17. Type **V** to select View report on screen (see Figure 6-15).

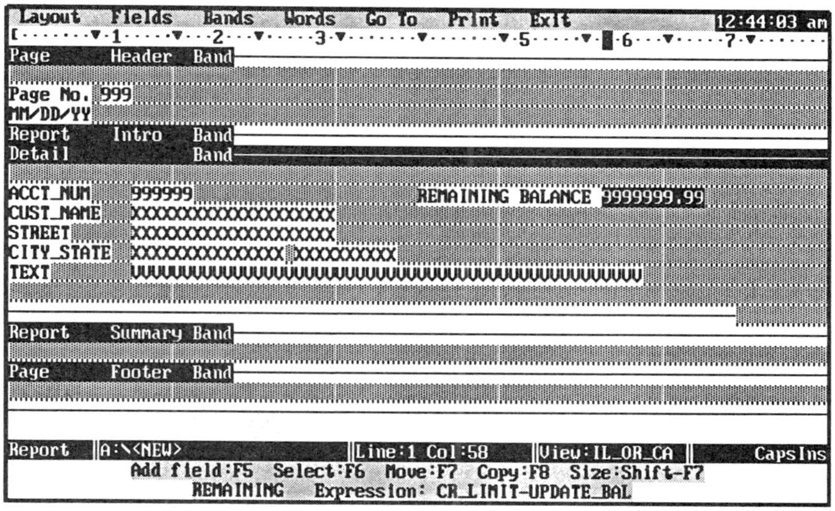

```
 Layout  Fields  Bands  Words  Go To  Print  Exit          12:44:03 am
[······▼·1·····▼·····2···▼····3·▼·····▼·······▼·5·····▼·■·6·▼···▼···7·▼·····
 Page     Header  Band
 Page No. 999
 MM/DD/YY
 Report   Intro   Band
 Detail           Band

 ACCT_NUM  999999                    REMAINING BALANCE 9999999.99
 CUST_NAME XXXXXXXXXXXXXXXXXXX
 STREET    XXXXXXXXXXXXXXXXXX
 CITY_STATE XXXXXXXXXXXXXX XXXXXXXXX
 TEXT       UUUUUUUUUUUUUUUUUUUUUUUUUUUUUUUUUUUUUUUUUUUUUU


 Report   Summary Band
 Page     Footer  Band

 Report   A:\<NEW>            Line:1 Col:58    View:IL_OR_CA      CapsIns
         Add field:F5  Select:F6  Move:F7  Copy:F8  Size:Shift-F7
              REMAINING   Expression: CR_LIMIT-UPDATE_BAL
```

Figure 6-14:
Placing a Calculated Field

```
 Page No.    1
 08/03/92

 ACCT_NUM    2145            REMAINING BALANCE    3850.00
 CUST_NAME   MURPHY
 STREET      23 OAK
 CITY_STATE  LEI, IL      78374
 TEXT        ALWAYS PAYS PROMPTLY.


 ACCT_NUM    4115            REMAINING BALANCE    2400.00
 CUST_NAME   BROWN
 STREET      100 ELM
 CITY_STATE  MAR, CA      95485
 TEXT        CREDIT IS EXCELLENT. NEVER USES FULL CREDIT LIMIT.


 ACCT_NUM    4155            REMAINING BALANCE    1700.00
 CUST_NAME   JONES
 STREET      345 ELM
            Cancel viewing: ESC,  Continue viewing: SPACEBAR
```

Memo fields print out on a report

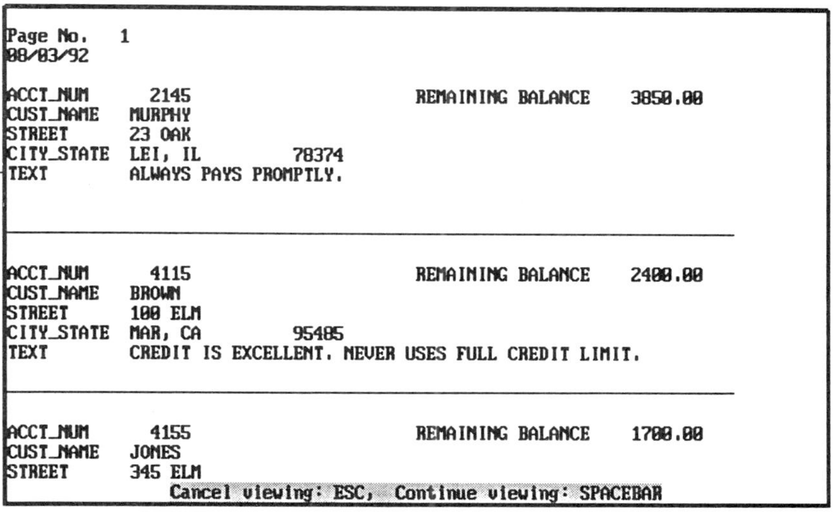

Figure 6-15:
Viewing the Form Design

18. Press the **[spacebar]** several times to return to the design screen.
    To save the design,
19. Press **[Alt]-[E]** to open the Exit menu.
20. Type **S** to select Save changes and exit.
21. Type the name **REM_BAL** and press **[Enter]**.
    After dBASE generates the report design, you will be returned to the Control Center.

Printing Labels

Creating a label design is similar to designing a form report. You place fields where desired within a frame that matches the size of the labels you will be using. The Status Bar shows the current cursor position.

You will create mailing labels for the records in the MASTER database. To create a label format for the MASTER file,

1.   Open MASTER for use so that it is above the horizontal line.
2.   Move the highlight bar on top of <create> in the Labels panel and press [**Enter**].

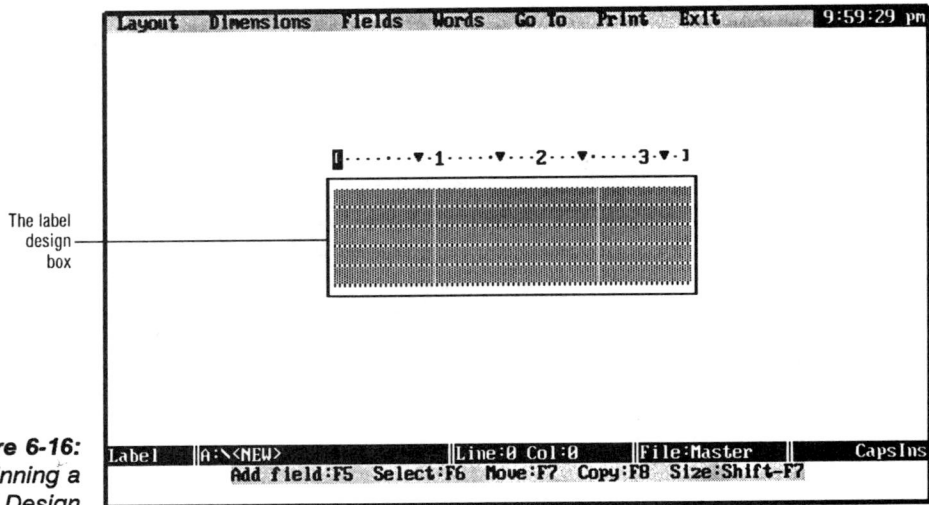

Figure 6-16:
Beginning a Label Design

The empty label design screen appears (as shown in Figure 6-16). A frame outlines the size of the default label (3 1/2 by 15/16). Several different predefined sizes are available in the Dimensions menu under Predefined Size. The remaining choices in the same menu allow you to create any size label desired. All placed fields and typed headings must fit within the frame. You must place each item on the design one by one.

To change the predefined label design to two labels side by side ("two up"),

1.   Press [**Alt**]-[**D**] to open the Dimensions menu.
2.   Type **P** to select Predefined Size.
3.   Press **2** to pick 15/16 x 3 1/2 by 2 (as shown in Figure 6-17). The same size frame remains on the label design screen, but dBASE will now place two labels side by side.
           To place the name and address fields,
4.   Press the down arrow [↓] to move onto Line:1 (the second line of the label).
           To select the first field, you could open the Fields menu and pick Add field; however, a quicker way is to press the [**F5**] key (as mentioned in the Navigation line).
5.   Press [**F5**] to open the pick list.
6.   Move the highlight bar on top of CUST_NAME, and press [**Enter**].

The field definition menu opens. You do not want to alter this field, so,

7. Press **[Ctrl]-[End]** to accept the definition.
    The field is placed on the design.

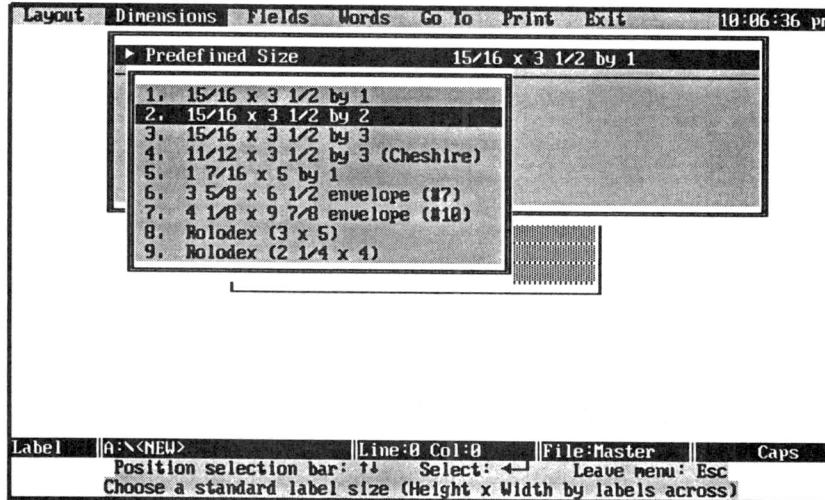

Figure 6-17:
Selecting the
Label Size

8. Press **[Enter]** to move to Line:2.
9. Repeat steps 5 through 8 to place the STREET field on the line below the name.
    The cursor should now be at Line:3 Col:0.
10. Press **[F5]** to open the pick list.
11. Move the highlight bar on top of CITY_STATE, and press **[Enter]**.
12. Press **[Ctrl]-[End]** to accept the definition.
    On the same line as the city and state you will place the ZIP code. There should be one or two spaces between the state and the ZIP code, so,
13. Press the **[spacebar]** twice.
    Typed spaces on a label (or report) are very important, for if they connect two fields, the fields will be printed that number of spaces apart no matter how short the first field is. This is called "trimming."
    To place the ZIP code field,
14. Press **[F5]** to open the picklist.
15. Move the highlight bar on top of ZIP and press **[Enter]**.
16. Press **[Ctrl]-[End]** to accept the definition.
    That completes the design (as shown in Figure 6-18).
    To preview the labels,
17. Press **[Alt]-[P]** to open the Print menu.
18. Type **V** to select View report on screen.
    The messages are similar to those on the report design screen as dBASE IV generates the program to produce the labels.

Notice that there are two mailing labels side by side, and that the ZIP code is always two spaces away from the state, no matter how long or short the city name is.

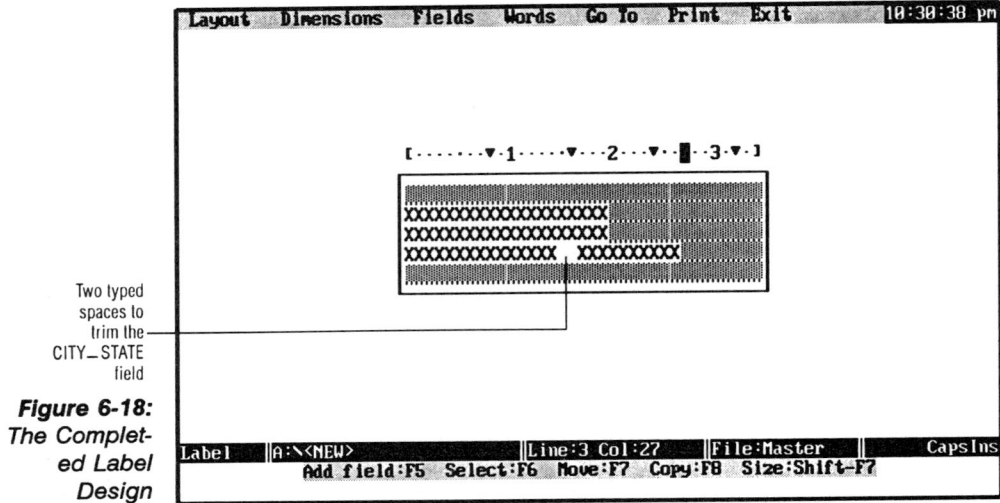

```
 Layout   Dimensions   Fields   Words   Go To   Print   Exit           10:30:38 pm



              [·······▼·1·····▼···2··▼··■··3·▼·]

              ┌─────────────────────────────────┐
              │░░░░░░░░░░░░░░░░░░░░░░             │
              │XXXXXXXXXXXXXXXXXX                 │
              │XXXXXXXXXXXXXXXXXX░░░░             │
              │XXXXXXXXXXXXXX  XXXXXXXXXX         │
              │░░░░░░░░░░░░░░░░░░░░░░             │
              └─────────────────────────────────┘




 Label    A:\<NEW>                  Line:3 Col:27    File:Master        CapsIns
          Add field:F5   Select:F6   Move:F7   Copy:F8   Size:Shift-F7
```

Two typed spaces to trim the CITY_STATE field

Figure 6-18: The Completed Label Design

19.   Press the **[spacebar]** enough times to return to the design screen.
       To save the design,
20.   Press **[Alt]-[E]** to open the Exit menu.
21.   Type **S** to select Save changes and exit.
22.   Type the name **MAILING** and press **[Enter]**.
       You will be returned to the Control Center after dBASE generates the label design program.
       To print the labels,
23.   Press **[Enter]** with the highlight bar on top of MAILING in the Labels panel.
24.   Type **P** to select Print label.
       In the pop-up print menu,
25.   Press **B** to Begin printing.

Observing Filenames Related to a Database

When you have created a report or label design for a database, the catalog moves that name above the line in the Reports or Labels panel whenever that database is opened and moves above the line. That way you will know which report or label designs go with which databases. The label design MAILING is related to MASTER, so it is currently above the line because MASTER is above the line.

To further observe this relationship,

1.   Move the highlight bar on top of MASTER (which is still above the line), and press **[Enter]**.
2.   Type **C** to select Close file.

Both MASTER and MAILING move below the line.
3.   Move the highlight bar on top of ARTRAN, and press **[Enter]**.
4.   Type **U** to select Use file.
     Both ARTRAN and ARREPORT move above the line (as shown in Figure 6-19).

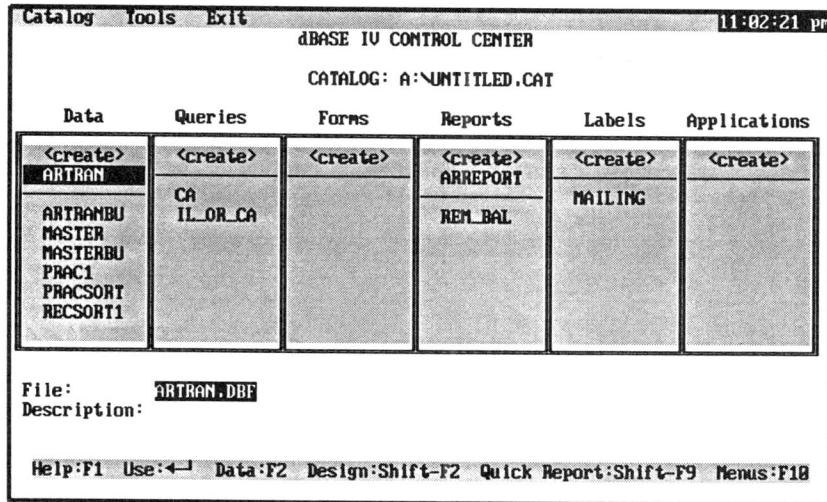

Figure 6-19:
Observing
Related Files

5.   Move the highlight bar on top of IL_OR_CA in the Queries panel, and press **[Enter]**.
6.   Type **U** to select Use view.
     Both IL_OR_CA and REM_BAL move above the line.
7.   Press **[Enter]** again and type C to close IL_OR_CA.
     Since no file is open, all names are below the line.

  You have now finished the exercises for Lesson 6. At this point, you can continue or quit. If you decide to quit, remember to exit properly from dBASE IV. Using the Quit to DOS option in the Exit menu automatically closes any open files.

Review Exercises

1.   List the steps necessary to design a report format.
2.   List the steps necessary to design a label format.
3.   Create a report format to print out the contents of your PRAC1 name and address file.
     A. Use a Quick layout; select Form layout.
     B. Open the Report Intro Band and enter the title CLUB ROSTER.
     C. Center the title.
     D. Switch the positions of the Page Header and Report Intro bands so that the Report Intro Band is on top.
     E. Remove the line containing the PHONE number field.
     F. Save the design.

G. Print the report.

4. Create and save a query that includes only the customer's name and the amount due for all records from PRAC1.

    A. Create a Column layout report for the resulting view.
    B. View the report on the screen, then return to the design screen.
    C. Insert a blank line above the sum for the AMOUNT_DUE column and draw a line above the sum.
    D. Save the design.
    E. Print the report.

7
Introduction to Programming

The objectives of this lesson are to write a simple program that will
- Append data
- Edit data
- Delete records
- Print labels using an existing label design

Programming in dBASE IV

Programming in dBASE IV is similar to performing a series of menu commands, except that the commands are written out. The program reads each command and executes it in sequence. The advantage of writing programs is that once they are typed and tested, with a few keystrokes you can execute a series of commands that you use frequently. Rather than selecting the various commands repeatedly, you simply run a program that has all of the commands already recorded in it.

As you proceed through this lesson, you will type a sample program using the dBASE program editor. You access the editor by choosing <create> in the Applications panel in the Control Center. The exercise will take you through various sections (modules) of a simple program and explain the fundamental commands used in each section.

Entering the Program Editor

dBASE IV uses a text editor to enter and save programming statements. Text editors have some of the basic features of word processing programs, such as word-wrap and insertion and deletion of text. Pressing **[Enter]** on <create> in the Applications panel and selecting "dBASE program" in the dialog box that follows activates the text editor.

To begin writing your database program,

1. Move the highlight bar on top of <create> in the Applications panel and press **[Enter]**.

2.   Type **D** to pick dBASE program (as shown in Figure 7-1).

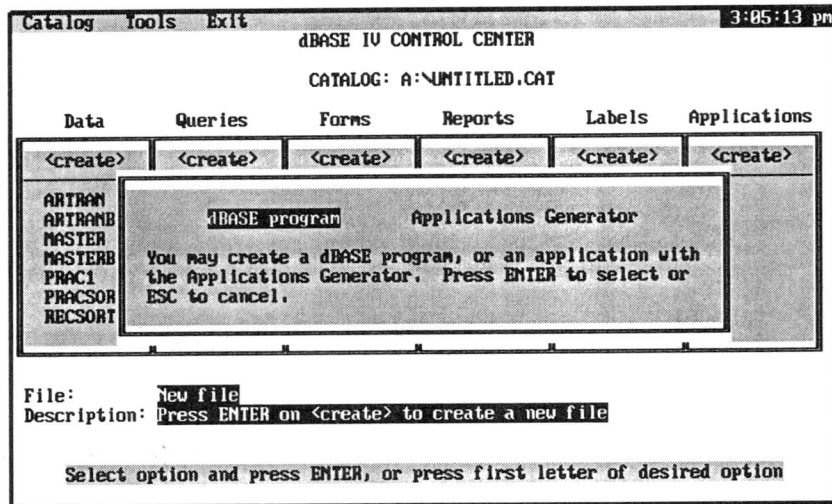

Figure 7-1:
Creating a
dBASE
Program

You will enter the program editor (as shown in Figure 7-2).

Figure 7-2:
The Program
Editor

Programs can be typed in any case, so
3.   Press **[CapsLock]** to turn off capital letters.

Creating Program Documentation

Program documentation, or comments in a program, records important information about the program. Documentation comments do not affect the execution of the program statements. Documentation comments are always preceded by an asterisk (*).

To create the program documentation, as shown in Figure 7-3, you will begin by naming your program and specifying the drive on which it is located. To enter the name and drive location of your program,

```
 Layout  Words  Go To  Print  Exit
 ▌·······▼1······▼··2·····▼····3··▼·······4▼·······▼5······▼··6····▼···7··▼·······
* Program...: A:ACCOUNTS.PRG
* Author....: Susan Student
* Date......: 9/18/92




 Program  A:\<NEW>                    Line:4 Col:1                          Ins
```

Figure 7-3:
Beginning the
Program

1.   Type *** Program...: A:ACCOUNTS.PRG** and press **[Enter]**.
     To enter your name,
2.   Type *** Author....: (YOUR NAME)** and press **[Enter]**.
     To enter the date when you created or revised the program,
3.   Type *** Date......: (TODAY'S DATE AS MM/DD/YY)** and press **[Enter]**.

Setting Up the Program Environment

After documenting the program, you will need to set up the program environment. To set up the program environment, you will specify default conditions for the program. Default conditions can range from screen colors to whether or not you want the bell to ring each time you exit a field on the screen.

dBASE IV uses SET commands to set the default conditions. These SET commands can be changed as needed in different sections of the program. To continue entering the program (you should still be in the program editor),

1.   Type **SET TALK OFF** and press **[Enter]**.
     The SET TALK OFF command prevents dBASE IV processing messages, such as "sorting 100% complete," from appearing and disrupting the screen's appearance.
2.   Type **SET BELL OFF** and press **[Enter]**.
     The SET BELL OFF command turns off the warning bell you would hear if you entered invalid data or if a field had been filled with data.
3.   Type **SET STATUS ON** and press **[Enter]**.

This command displays the status bar on the screen.

4. Type **SET ESCAPE OFF** and press **[Enter]**.

   This command disables the **[Esc]** key so that users cannot exit from a program prematurely or discontinue a program in process.

5. Type **SET CONFIRM ON** and press **[Enter]**.

   CONFIRM ON prevents the cursor from moving automatically to the next field.

Retrieving a Data File

After you have set up the program environment, you will retrieve the MASTER file. You will then begin to create a menu display.

To retrieve the MASTER file,

1. Type **USE A:MASTER** and press **[Enter]**.

   The USE command opens the MASTER database file stored on the disk in drive A.

2. Type **DO WHILE .T.** and press **[Enter]**.

   The DO WHILE .T. statement allows the program to continue executing in a never-ending loop until you select the Quit option from the menu. Anytime you write a DO WHILE statement, you must also include an ENDDO statement near the bottom or end of the program.

3. Type *___**Display menu options, centered on the screen** and press **[Enter]**.

4. Type *___**Draw menu border and print heading** and press **[Enter]**.

   These two comment lines describe the following section of the program.

Creating a Menu

The following program statements will create and display a menu when the program is executed. The menu will consist of six choices. Programming statements use line and column numbers to control the location of the menu choices on the screen. The SAY statements create "display only" fields that can display text or data on the screen. The GET statements display fields on the screen but also allow you to enter data into those fields.

NOTE: Whenever the program requests a O (number), use a zero (0).

To write a statement that will clear the screen for the menu display,

1. Type **CLEAR** and press **[Enter]**.

   To draw a double-line from screen line 2, column 0 to screen line 15, column 79,

2. Type @ **2,0 TO 15,79 DOUBLE** and press **[Enter]**.

To display the words "MAIN MENU" starting at screen line 3, column 31,

3. Type @ **3,31 SAY [M A I N M E N U]** and press **[Enter]**.

In dBASE, square brackets ([and]) can substitute for quotation marks.

To draw another double line below MAIN MENU from screen line 4, column 1 to screen line 4, column 78,

4. Type @ **4,1 TO 4,78 DOUBLE** and press **[Enter]**.

To display the words " 1. ADD INFORMATION" at screen line 7, column 30,

5. Type @ **7,30 SAY [1. ADD INFORMATION]** and press **[Enter]**.

To display the words "2. CHANGE INFORMATION" starting at screen line 8, column 30,

6. Type @ **8,30 SAY [2. CHANGE INFORMATION]** and press **[Enter]**.

To display the words "3. REMOVE INFORMATION" starting at screen line 9, column 30,

7. Type @ **9,30 SAY [3. REMOVE INFORMATION]** and press **[Enter]**.

To display the words "4. REVIEW INFORMATION" starting at screen line 10, column 30,

8. Type @ **10,30 SAY [4. REVIEW INFORMATION]** and press **[Enter]**.

To display the words "5. PRINT LABELS" starting at screen line 11, column 30,

9. Type @ **11,30 SAY [5. PRINT LABELS]** and press **[Enter]**.

To display the words "0. EXIT" starting at screen line 13, column 30,

10. Type @ **13,30 SAY [0. EXIT]** and press **[Enter]**.

The next command stores the value of 0 to a variable named selectnum. The field selectnum will be used as the data entry field for the menu choices when the program is executed. To enter this command,

11. Type **STORE 0 TO selectnum** and press **[Enter]**.

To display the word "select" starting at screen line 15, column 33,

12. Type @ **15,33 SAY " select "** and press **[Enter]**.

The next command places the data entry field, selectnum, on the screen at line 15, column 42. The PICTURE 9 clause will only allow you to enter single digit numbers into the selectnum field. The RANGE 0,5 limits the numbers that can be entered to 0, 1, 2, 3, 4 or 5. To enter this command,

13. Type @ **15,42 GET selectnum PICTURE "9" RANGE 0,5** and press **[Enter]**.

The next command reads the data entered into the selectnum variable so that the DO case in the next line can transfer the execution of the program to the corresponding program module. To enter this command,

14.   Type **READ** and press **[Enter]**.

Entering the Active Parts of the Program

The following sections are distinct program segments (modules). Each segment performs a specific task such as adding records to a file, updating records in a file, and deleting records in a file. This program is divided into these segments to make it easier to follow the logic and locate program errors.

Exit Section

In this portion of the program, you will enter commands that will be executed when you exit the program. To enter this portion of the program, you will begin with the DO CASE command. The DO CASE command sets up a conditional branch. The program will begin the branch with the first DO CASE command and will check the contents of the selectnum field each time it passes through the branch. The contents of the selectnum field determines which set of CASE statements is executed (which branch is taken).

To begin entering this section (you should still be in the program editor),

1.   Type **DO CASE** and press **[Enter]**.
   To specify that if you enter a 0 on the Main Menu, the following commands in this section will be executed,
2.   Type **CASE selectnum = 0** and press **[Enter]**.
   To set the bell back to on status, so that the exit module will set the environment back to the original preprogram settings,
3.   Type **SET BELL ON** and press **[Enter]**.
   To allow dBASE IV to display processing messages,
4.   Type **SET TALK ON** and press **[Enter]**.
   To close all databases,
5.   Type **CLOSE ALL** and press **[Enter]**.
   To end the program run and return to the Control Center,
6.   Type **RETURN** and press **[Enter]**.

Append Section

In this section, you will enter commands that allow you to append data onto a database file.

To specify that if you select a 1 at the Main Menu the following commands in this section will be executed,

1.   Type **CASE selectnum = 1** and press **[Enter]**.
   To enter the comment line that identifies the module,
2.   Type *** DO ADD INFORMATION** and press **[Enter]**.
   To enter the dBASE command used to add records to the file,
3.   Type **APPEND** and press **[Enter]**.

To have the cursor move automatically to the next field when the current field is filled,

4. Type **SET CONFIRM OFF** and press **[Enter]**.

The next command stores a blank (one space which is typed between a pair of quotation marks) to a variable named wait_subst. Wait_subst is a memory variable field created by dBASE. The field stores the value entered in the following GET command. To enter this command,

5. Type **STORE " " TO wait_subst** and press **[Enter]**.

To display the message "Press any key to continue" on the screen and have dBASE wait until you press a key before returning to the Main Menu,

6. Type **@ 23,0 SAY "Press any key to continue..." GET wait_subst** and press **[Enter]**.

The value of the key to be pressed is stored in the memory variable wait_subst.

To have dBASE process the data entered,

7. Type **READ** and press **[Enter]**.

To prevent the cursor from moving automatically to the next field,

8. Type **SET CONFIRM ON** and press **[Enter]**.

Edit Section

In this section, you will enter commands that will allow you to edit your database file. To specify that if you select a 2 at the Main Menu, the following commands in this section will be executed,

1. Type **CASE selectnum = 2** and press **[Enter]**.

To enter the comment that describes the edit module,

2. Type *** DO CHANGE INFORMATION** and press **[Enter]**.

To position the record pointer at the top of the file,

3. Type **GOTO TOP** and press **[Enter]**.

To enter the dBASE command used to edit records in a file,

4. Type **EDIT** and press **[Enter]**.

To have the cursor move automatically to the next field when the current field is filled,

5. Type **SET CONFIRM OFF** and press **[Enter]**.

To store a blank to a variable named wait_subst,

6. Type **STORE " " TO wait_subst** and press **[Enter]**.

The next command displays the message "Press any key to continue" on the screen and waits until a key is pressed before returning to the Main Menu. To enter the command,

7. Type **@ 23,0 SAY "Press any key to continue" GET wait_subst** and press **[Enter]**.

To have dBASE process the data entered,

8. Type **READ** and press **[Enter]**.

To prevent the cursor from moving automatically to the next field,

9.   Type **SET CONFIRM ON** and press [**Enter**].

Pack Module

In this section, you will enter commands that allow you to pack, or remove records from, the database file.

To specify that if you select a 3 at the Main Menu, the following commands in this section will be executed,

1.   Type **CASE selectnum = 3** and press [**Enter**].
To enter the comment that describes the module,
2.   Type *** DO REMOVE INFORMATION** and press [**Enter**].
To position the record pointer to the top of the file,
3.   Type **GOTO TOP** and press [**Enter**].
To allow dBASE to display processing messages,
4.   Type **SET TALK ON** and press [**Enter**].
To clear the screen,
5.   Type **CLEAR** and press [**Enter**].
To enter the two commands that will display the packing message on the screen,
6.   Type **@ 2,0 SAY** " " and press [**Enter**].
7.   Type **? "PACKING DATABASE TO REMOVE RECORDS MARKED FOR DELETION"** and press [**Enter**].
To run the pack command,
8.   Type **PACK** and press [**Enter**].
To prevent dBASE from displaying processing messages,
9.   Type **SET TALK OFF** and press [**Enter**].
To have the cursor move automatically to the next field when the current field is filled,
10.   Type **SET CONFIRM OFF** and press [**Enter**].
To store a blank to a variable named wait_subst,
11.   Type **STORE** " " **TO wait_subst** and press [**Enter**].
To have dBASE display the message "Press any key to continue" on the screen and wait until you press a key before returning to the Main Menu,
12.   Type **@ 23,0 SAY "Press any key to continue" GET wait_subst** and press [**Enter**].
To have dBASE process the data entered,
13.   Type **READ** and press [**Enter**].
To prevent the cursor from moving automatically to the next field,
14.   Type **SET CONFIRM ON** and press [**Enter**].

Browse Module

In this section, you will enter commands that will allow you to use Browse mode.

To specify that if you select a 4 at the Main Menu, the following commands in this section will be executed,

1. Type **CASE selectnum = 4** and press **[Enter]**.
   To enter the comment that describes the module,
2. Type *** DO REVIEW INFORMATION** and press **[Enter]**.
   To position the record pointer at the top of the file,
3. Type **GOTO TOP** and press **[Enter]**.
   To run the dBASE Browse command,
4. Type **BROWSE** and press **[Enter]**.
   To have the cursor move automatically to the next field when the current field is filled,
5. Type **SET CONFIRM OFF** and press **[Enter]**.
   To store a blank to a variable named wait_subst,
6. Type **STORE " " TO wait_subst** and press **[Enter]**.
   To display the message "Press any key to continue..." on the screen and have dBASE wait until you press a key before returning to the Main Menu,
7. Type **@ 23,0 SAY "Press any key to continue..." GET wait_subst** and press **[Enter]**.
   To have dBASE process the data entered,
8. Type **READ** and press **[Enter]**.
   To prevent the cursor from moving automatically to the next field,
9. Type **SET CONFIRM ON** and press **[Enter]**.

Print Report Section

In this section, you will enter commands that will allow you to print labels.

To specify that if you select 5 at the Main Menu, the following commands in this section will be executed,

1. Type **CASE selectnum = 5** and press **[Enter]**.
   To enter the comment that describes the module,
2. Type *** DO PRINT LABELS** and press **[Enter]**.
   To position the record pointer to the top of the file,
3. Type **GOTO TOP** and press **[Enter]**.
   To have dBASE set the label design to MAILING and send the output to the printer,
4. Type **REPORT LABEL FORM A:MAILING TO PRINT** and press **[Enter]**.
   To have the cursor move automatically to the next field when the current field is filled,
5. Type **SET CONFIRM OFF** and press **[Enter]**.
   To store a blank to a variable named wait_subst,
6. Type **STORE " " TO wait_subst** and press **[Enter]**.
   To display the message "Turn printer off before proceeding,"
7. Type **@ 22,0 SAY "Turn off printer before proceeding"** and press **[Enter]**.

To display the message "Press any key to continue" and have dBASE wait until you press a key before returning to the Main Menu,

8. Type @ **23,0 SAY "Press any key to continue" GET wait_subst** and press [**Enter**].

To process the data entered,

9. Type **READ** and press [**Enter**].

To prevent the cursor from moving automatically to the next field,

10. Type **SET CONFIRM ON** and press [**Enter**].

To specify the end point for the DO CASE command,

11. Type **ENDCASE** and press [**Enter**].

To specify the end point for the DO WHILE command,

12. Type **ENDDO** and press [**Enter**].

To close all databases,

13. Type **CLOSE ALL** and press [**Enter**].

To end the program run and return to the Control Center,

14. Type **RETURN** and press [**Enter**].

To enter the comment that identifies the end of the program (End Of File),

15. Type *** EOF: A:ACCOUNTS.PRG** and press [**Enter**].

To save the program,

16. Open the Exit menu and pick Save changes and exit.

17. Type the name **ACCOUNTS** in the Save as: box and press [**Enter**].

The extension for a program is automatically **.PRG**. To run the program,

18. Move the highlight on top of ACCOUNTS and press [**Enter**].

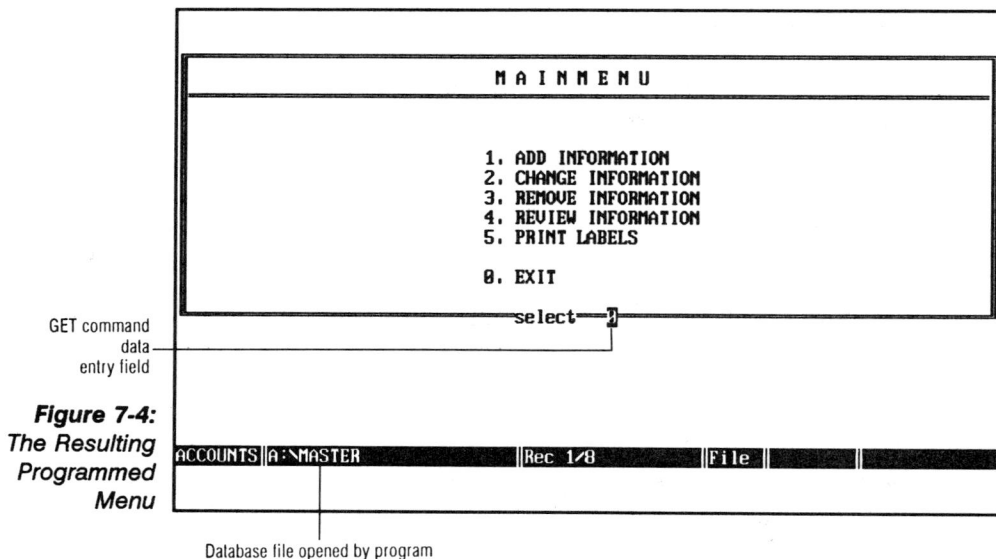

GET command
data
entry field

Figure 7-4:
*The Resulting
Programmed
Menu*

Database file opened by program

19.   Type **R** to select Run application, and press **Y** to answer Yes to
        "Are you sure you want to run this application?"

        After a message about compiling (translating into machine
        form), the program should draw its menu screen.

  You should see the menu shown in Figure 7-4. If the menu does not
appear and/or you get an error message, follow the steps below to
correct the programming error. (You will probably have several errors
at first.) Make all selections from the menu, starting with 1. ADD
INFORMATION, to ensure that the program contains no errors.

Reading Program Error Messages

As you attempt to run the program you have created, you will most
likely see error messages that indicate some slight entry errors. An
error message looks like the message shown in Figure 7-5.

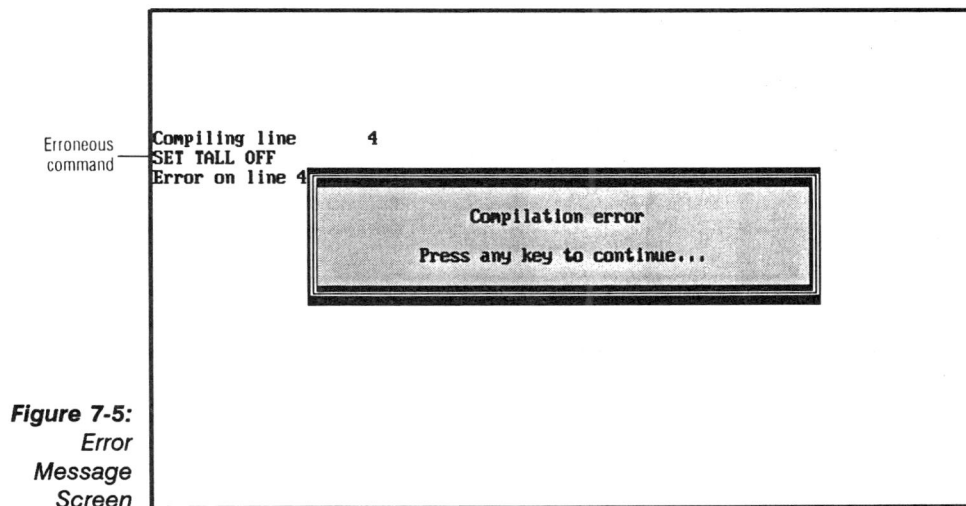

Erroneous command

```
Compiling line        4
SET TALL OFF
Error on line 4
```

Compilation error

Press any key to continue...

Figure 7-5:
*Error
Message
Screen*

  If you should receive a program error message,

1.   Follow the error message by pressing any key or typing **C** to
        cancel the program run.
        You should return to the Control Center.
2.   Press **[Enter]** on top of the filename.
3.   Type **M** to pick Modify application.
4.   Go to the line in the program in which the error occurred,
        according to the error message.
        Look at the printout of the program at the end of this lesson to
        determine where your error is.
5.   Correct the error.
        If the error involves a command that is missing entirely, rather
        than one that was simply mistyped, you will need to insert a line

and then enter the missing command on this inserted line. To insert the line, position the cursor at the end of the line under which you want the new line to appear (if you position the cursor in the middle of a line, you will divide the line in half) and,

6. Press **[Ctrl]-N**.
7. Add the command.
8. Use the Exit menu to save your correction(s).
9. Run the program again.
   The program will either run and the menu will appear, or another error message will appear. Using steps 1-7, correct all errors until your program runs error free.

Below is an annotated copy of ACCOUNTS.PRG. To compare your program with this copy, you can print a copy of your ACCOUNTS.PRG program. To do so,

1. Move the highlight bar on top of ACCOUNTS and press **[Enter]**.
2. Type **M** to pick Modify application.
3. Press **[Alt]-[P]** to open the Print menu.
4. Type **B** to select Begin printing.
   Be sure that the printer is connected and turned on.
5. Exit to the Control Center.

The program will print out as follows (indentations have been added for clarity and are not necessary in your program):

```
* Program...: A:ACCOUNTS.PRG
* Author....: (Your Name)
* Date......: (Today's Date)

SET TALK OFF
SET BELL OFF
SET STATUS ON
SET ESCAPE OFF
SET CONFIRM ON
USE A:MASTER
DO WHILE .T.
    *__Display menu options, centered on the screen
    *__Draw menu border and print heading
    CLEAR
    @ 2,0 TO 15,79 DOUBLE
    @ 3,31 SAY [MAIN MENU]
    @ 4,1 TO 4,78 DOUBLE
    @ 7,30 SAY [1. ADD INFORMATION]
    @ 8,30 SAY [2. CHANGE INFORMATION]
    @ 9,30 SAY [3. REMOVE INFORMATION]
    @ 10,30 SAY [4. REVIEW INFORMATION]
```

```
@ 11,30 SAY [5. PRINT LABELS]
@ 13,30 SAY [0. EXIT]
STORE 0 TO selectnum
@ 15,33 SAY " select "
@ 15,42 GET selectnum PICTURE "9" RANGE 0,5
READ

DO CASE
   CASE selectnum = 0
   SET BELL ON
   SET TALK ON
   CLOSE ALL
   RETURN
   CASE selectnum = 1
   * DO ADD INFORMATION
   APPEND
   SET CONFIRM OFF
   STORE " " TO wait_subst
   @ 23,0 SAY "Press any key to continue..." GET wait_subst
   READ
   SET CONFIRM ON
   CASE selectnum = 2
   * DO CHANGE INFORMATION
   GOTO TOP
   EDIT
   SET CONFIRM OFF
   STORE " " TO wait_subst
   @ 23,0 SAY "Press any key to continue..." GET wait_subst
   READ
   SET CONFIRM ON
   CASE selectnum = 3
   * DO REMOVE INFORMATION
   GOTO TOP
   SET TALK ON
   CLEAR
   @ 2,0 say " "
   ? 'PACKING DATABASE TO REMOVE RECORDS MARKED FOR
   DELETION'
   PACK
   SET TALK OFF
   SET CONFIFM OFF
   STORE " " TO wait_subst
   @ 23,0 SAY "Press any key to continue..." GET wait_subst
   READ
   SET CONFIRM ON
   CASE selectnum = 4
   * DO REVIEW INFORMATION
   GOTO TOP
```

```
      BROWSE
      SET CONFIRM OFF
      STORE " " TO wait_subst
      @ 23,0 SAY "Press any key to continue..." GET wait_subst
      READ
      SET CONFIRM ON
      CASE selectnum = 5
      * DO PRINT LABELS
      GOTO TOP
      LABEL FORM MAILING TO PRINT
      SET CONFIRM OFF
      STORE " " TO wait_subst
      @ 22,0 SAY "Turn off printer before proceeding"
      @ 23,0 SAY "Press any key to continue..." GET wait_subst
      READ
      SET CONFIRM ON
ENDCASE
ENDDO
CLOSE ALL
RETURN
* EOF: A:ACCOUNTS.PRG
```

You have now finished the exercises for Lesson 7. At this point, you can continue or quit. If you decide to quit, remember to exit properly because failure to close the files before turning the computer off can result in lost data! The Quit to DOS option in the Exit menu automatically closes the open files.

Review Exercises
Because of the complex nature of the program created in this lesson, there are no review exercises.

APPENDIX
A: Home Inventory Project

A: Lesson 1

The Home Inventory Project creates a database of personal assets. The date field contains the date the item was purchased. The description and serial number of the asset are captured in the next two fields. The category field contains a general group name that describes the item. The cost field contains the original purchase price of the inventoried item.

Note: If you have been using the same 5 1/4 inch low-density (360K) diskette for all of the exercises in this book, obtain a fresh diskette before beginning these projects. The old diskette may be filling up.

1. Create a database from the Control Center using the record structure given in Table A-1 below. Name the database file HOME_INV.

Field Number	Field Name	Field Type	Width	Dec	Index
1	DATE	D	8		N
2	DESCRIPT	C	20		N
3	SERIAL_NUM	C	12		N
4	CATEGORY	C	10		N
5	COST	N	7	2	N

Table A-1

2. Print the record structure for the file HOME_INV.
3. Add the 10 records listed in Table A-2 to the HOME_INV

database file.

4.   Display the 10 records in HOME_INV on the Browse screen.
5.   Make a back-up copy of HOME_INV.DBF called HOMEBU.DBF and verify that the copy command was successfully executed.
6.   Add the database file HOMEBU.DBF to the catalog.
7.   Close all files.

DATE	DESCRIPTION	SERIAL NUMBER	CATEGORY	COST
06/30/87	REFRIGERATOR	098-456ACZ	APPLIANCE	989.00
12/15/87	COMPUTER	195C3028	OFFICE	2,400.00
02/14/88	DIAMOND NECKLACE	983CC	JEWELRY	3,000.00
07/23/88	WASHING MACHINE	195834-2	APPLIANCE	517.25
03/03/89	COMPACT DISK PLAYER	RCB126	ELECTRONIC	299.59
12/22/89	SOFA	3925610Z	FURNITURE	639.95
01/10/90	TELEVISION	7-394568	ELECTRONIC	299.59
05/16/90	RECLINER	14-000-B783	FURNITURE	339.27
10/15/91	TYPEWRITER	893612	OFFICE	219.85
09/06/92	14K GOLD EARRINGS	1439Z	JEWELRY	79.35

Table A-2

A: Lesson 2

Perform the following operations:

1.   Open (use) the database file HOME_INV.
2.   Modify the record structure of HOME_INV by adding a memo field called TEXT. Change the width of the DESCRIPT field from 20 characters to 25 characters. Print a copy of the new record structure.
3.   In Edit mode, position the record pointer at the top of the file. Press **[PgDn]** to move to record 2. Add the following memo notation to record 2: INSURED FOR REPLACEMENT COST THROUGH STATE FIRE & CASUALTY CO.
4.   Position the record pointer at record 10. Change the description to: 14K GOLD DIAMOND EARRINGS.
5.   Display all records in the database file HOME_INV in Browse mode.
6.   Mark the "TYPEWRITER" record for deletion.
7.   Erase the marked record.
8.   Mark the "RCB126" record for deletion.
9.   Clear the deletion mark from "RCB126."
10.   Close the HOME_INV file.

A: Lesson 3

Perform the following operations:

1.   Open the database file HOME_INV.
2.   Create a query based on HOME_INV. Set the criterion to include all items in the JEWELRY Category. View the result.
3.   Change the query to set the criterion to include all items priced below $500.00. View the result.
4.   Change the query to set the criterion to include all items priced above $750.00 and purchased prior to 1990. View the result.
5.   Change the query to set the criterion to include all items whose serial number contains a dash. Remove all fields from the View Skeleton and include only the description and serial number fields. View the result.
6.   Save the query as DASHES.
7.   Close all files.

A: Lesson 4

Perform the following operations:

1.   Open the database file HOME_INV.
2.   Sort the database file HOME_INV into alphabetical order by CATEGORY. Name the sorted file HOME1SRT.
3.   Display all of the records in HOME1SRT in Browse mode.
4.   Sort the database file HOME_INV by CATEGORY and DATE. Name the sorted file HOME2SRT.
5.   Display all of the records in HOME2SRT in Browse mode.
6.   Make a back-up copy of HOME2SRT and verify that the copy was successfully executed.
7.   Create an index for HOME_INV based on the CATEGORY field and name the index CATEGORY. View the data in Browse mode to check that the index was correctly executed.
8.   Create an index for HOME_INV based on the CATEGORY and DESCRIPT fields simultaneously, and name the index CAT_DESC. View the data in Browse mode to check that the index was correctly executed.
9.   Switch back to the CATEGORY index and view the data.
10. Add the following record to the database file HOME_INV.
     DATE: 9/25/92
     DESCRIPT: MICROWAVE OVEN
     SERIAL_NUM: 98235-90
     CATEGORY: APPLIANCE
     COST: 259.85
11. View the data in Browse mode to check that the index correctly placed the new record.
12. Close all files.

A: Lesson 5

Perform the following operations:

1. Open the database file HOME_INV.
2. Use the Browse option to add the following two records to the database file:
    DATE: 10/26/92
    DESCRIPT: WALL UNIT
    SERIAL_NUM: 3409
    CATEGORY: FURNITURE
    COST: 2,080.88
    DATE: 10/30/92
    DESCRIPT: BEDROOM SET
    SERIAL_NUM: 9023-0
    CATEGORY: FURNITURE
    COST: 3,089.12
3. Use the Browse option to change the SERIAL_NUM for record 3 from 983CC to 98300.
4. Create a query to mark all FURNITURE for deletion. Perform the update, but do NOT erase the marked records.
5. View the database on the Browse screen and check for the Del denoting the marked records in the Status Bar.
6. Use the "Unmark all records" selection in the Organize menu on the Browse screen to unmark all records.
7. Use a Replace query to change the word "APPLIANCE" to "APPLIANCES" in the CATEGORY field. View the new data.
8. Abandon the query without saving it.
9. Close all files.

A: Lesson 6

Perform the following operations:

1. Create a Column report for HOME_INV. Use a Quick layout to get started.
2. Erase the memo field from the report design by moving the highlight on top of the TEXT field in the Detail Band and selecting Remove field in the Fields menu. Also, erase the column heading (TEXT).
3. Add a blank line above the sum in the Report Summary Band and draw a line above the sum.
4. Fix the right margin at 78 characters.
5. Open the Report Intro Band and add the report title INVENTORY LIST. Center the title.
6. Switch the positions of the Page Header Band and the Report Intro Band by selecting Page heading in report intro in the Bands menu.
7. View the report on the screen.

8. Save the report format as HOME_RPT.
9. Print the HOME_RPT report.
10. Close all files.

A: Lesson 7

These projects will demonstrate that a well-written program can be adapted for many applications.

Create a program to append, edit, browse, delete records, and print a report for the HOME_INV file. You will use the program that you created in Lesson 7 by copying it to another program and making changes to the new program.

1. On the DOS util screen, copy ACCOUNTS.PRG to the new name PROJ_1.PRG.
2. Add the PROJ_1 program to the Applications task panel. (Use the Catalog menu and remember to place the highlight in the Applications panel prior to opening the menu.) Use the description "ACCOUNTS PROGRAM MODIFIED FOR PROJECT 1."
3. With the highlight on top of PROJ_1.PRG, press **[Enter]** and select Modify application to enter the program editor.
4. Change the following:
    A. Change the name of the program in the Documentation Section.
    B. Change the name of the database in the Program Environment to A:HOME_INV.DBF.
    C. Change the label command in the Print Labels Module so that it will print a report instead by changing it to REPORT FORM A:HOME_RPT TO PRINT. Also change the menu choice number 5 to say "PRINT REPORT" instead of PRINT LABELS.
5. Save these changes.
6. Run PROJ_1.PRG.
7. Add three records.
8. Edit all of the records.
9. Using Browse or Edit mode, mark one record for deletion.
10. Pack the database file to erase the marked record.
11. Print a report.
12. Return to the DOS prompt.

APPENDIX
B: Personal Checkbook Project

B: Lesson 1

This project involves creating a personal checkbook register to record deposits and checks. Check numbers and deposit numbers are recorded as transaction numbers. The transaction type is recorded as a "D" for deposit or a "C" for check. The information in the payee field reflects to whom the check is written. The amount field contains the dollar amount of the check. Information concerning the reason for the transaction is recorded in the purpose field. The last field contains a "Y" for yes or an "N" for no to denote whether the transaction should be flagged for use in computing income taxes.

1. Create a database using the record structure format given in Table B-1 below. Name the database file CHECKBK.

Field Number	Field Name	Field Type	Width	Dec	Index
1	TRAN_NUM	N	4	0	N
2	TRAN_TYPE	C	1		N
3	TRAN_DATE	D	8		N
4	PAYEE	C	20		N
5	AMOUNT	N	7	2	N
6	PURPOSE	C	15		N
7	TAXES	C	1		N

Table B-1

2. Print the record structure for CHECKBK.

3. Add the 10 records listed in Table B-2 to the CHECKBK database file.
4. Display the 10 records in Browse mode.
5. Make a back-up copy of CHECKBK, naming it CHECKBK2, and verify that the copy was successfully executed.
6. Add CHECKBK2 to the catalog.
7. Close all files.

TRAN_NUM	TRAN_TYPE	TRAN_DATE	PAYEE	AMOUNT	PURPOSE	TAXES
1480	D	06/05/92	DEPOSIT	1,500.00	ROYALTY	Y
2273	C	06/22/92	SUPERMARKET INC.	33.48	GROCERIES	N
2274	C	06/22/92	KIDS TODAY	140.00	CHILD CARE	Y
2275	C	06/23/92	GAS TO GO	25.00	GASOLINE	Y
2276	C	06/24/92	CHARGE-IT, INC	89.00	PAYMENT	N
1481	D	06/25/92	DEPOSIT	750.00	PAYCHECK	N
2278	C	06/26/92	KATIE ISHAM	10.00	BIRTHDAY	N
2279	C	06/27/92	KIDS TODAY	140.00	CHILD CARE	Y
2280	C	06/28/92	UNITED HELP FUND	50.00	CHARITY	Y
2281	C	06/30/92	FIRST BANK	550.00	MORTGAGE	Y

Table B-2

B: Lesson 2

Perform the following operations:

1. Open the database file CHECKBK.
2. Modify the record structure of CHECKBK by adding a memo field called NOTES. Change the width of the PAYEE field from 20 characters to 25 characters. Print a copy of the new record structure.
3. On the Edit or Browse screen, add the following memo notations:
    Record 2: GROCERIES FOR CAMPING TRIP. CHARGE MARY AND SALLY ONE-THIRD OF THE BILL.
    Record 4: GASOLINE FOR CAMPING TRIP. CHARGE MARY AND SALLY ONE-THIRD OF THE BILL.
    Record 9: BEING DISTRICT REPRESENTATIVE, SALLY COLLECTED THE CHECK.
4. Change the contents of the PAYEE field on record 9 to: UNITED HELP ORGANIZATION.
5. Display the records in the CHECKBK file in Browse mode.
6. Mark the "KATIE ISHAM" record for deletion.
7. Erase the marked record.
8. Mark transaction number 2274 for deletion.
9. Clear the deletion mark from transaction number 2274.

10.   Close the CHECKBK file.

B: Lesson 3

Perform the following operations:

1.   Open the database file CHECKBK.
2.   Create a query based on CHECKBK. Set the criterion to include all DEPOSITs in the PAYEE field. View the result.
3.   Change the query to set the criterion to include all transactions (checks and deposits) larger than $100.00. View the result.
4.   Change the query to set the criterion to include only checks (not deposits) that are larger than $100.00. View the result.
5.   Change the query to set the criterion to include all items that are either a DEPOSIT or are made out to KIDS TODAY. Remove all fields from the View skeleton and include only the date, payee, and amount fields. View the result.
6.   Change the query to set the criterion to include all items whose PURPOSE begins with PAY. Remove all fields from the View Skeleton and include only the payee, amount, and purpose fields. View the result.
7.   Save the query with the name PAY.
8.   Close all files.

B: Lesson 4

Perform the following operations:

1.   Open the database file CHECKBK.
2.   Sort the database file CHECKBK into alphabetical order by PURPOSE. Name the sorted file CHK1SRT.
3.   Display all of the records in CHK1SRT in Browse mode.
4.   Sort the CHECKBK file by PAYEE and TRAN_DATE. Name the sorted file CHK2SRT.
5.   Display all of the records in CHK2SRT.
6.   Make a back-up copy of CHK2SRT. Verify that the copy was successfully executed and add the new database to the catalog.
7.   Create an index for CHECKBK based on the AMOUNT field and name the index AMOUNT. View the data in Browse mode to check that the index was correctly executed.
8.   Create an index for CHECKBK based on the PURPOSE field and name the index PURPOSE. View the data in Browse mode to check that the index was correctly executed.
9.   Switch back to the AMOUNT index and view the data.
10.   Switch to Natural Order and view the data.
11.   Create an index for CHECKBK based on PAYEE and name the index PAYEE. View the data.
12.   Add the following record to the CHECKBK file:
      TRANSACTION NUMBER: 2282

TRANSACTION TYPE: C
TRANSACTION DATE: 06/30/92
PAYEE: GAS TO GO
AMOUNT: 18.50
PURPOSE: GASOLINE
TAXES: Y

13. View the data in Browse mode to check that the index correctly placed the new record.
14. Close all files.

B: Lesson 5

Perform the following operations:

1. Open the database file CHECKBK. Order the records by the AMOUNT.
2. Use Browse mode to add the following two records to the CHECKBK file:
   TRAN_NUM: 2283
   TRAN_TYPE: C
   TRAN_DATE: 07/15/92
   PAYEE: SUPERMARKET, INC.
   AMOUNT: 74.12
   PURPOSE: GROCERIES
   TAXES: N
   TRAN_NUM: 2284
   TRAN_TYPE: C
   TRAN_DATE: 07/15/92
   PAYEE: KIDS TODAY
   AMOUNT: 140.00
   PURPOSE: DAY CARE
   TAXES: Y
3. Use Browse mode to change the PAYEE named FIRST BANK to FIRST REGIONAL BANK.
4. Create a query to mark for deletion all checks whose TRAN_NUM is smaller than 2275. Perform the update, but do NOT erase the marked records.
5. View the database on the Browse screen and check for the Del denoting the marked records in the Status Bar.
6. Use the "Unmark all records" selection in the Organize menu on the Browse screen to unmark all records.
7. Use a Replace query to change the words "CHILD CARE" to "DAY CARE" in the PURPOSE field. Examine the new data.
8. Use a Replace query to change the amount of each check for KIDS TODAY to $150.00. View the new values.
9. Abandon the query without saving it.
10. Close all files.

B: Lesson 6

Perform the following operations:

1. Create a Column report for CHECKBK. Use a Quick layout to get started.
2. Erase the last three fields (PURPOSE, TAXES, and NOTES) from the report design by moving the highlight on top of each field in the Detail Band and selecting Remove field in the Fields menu. Also, erase the three column headings.
3. Erase the field for the SUM of the TRAN_NUM column from the Report Summary Band.
4. Add a blank line above the remaining sum in the Report Summary Band and draw a line above the sum.
5. Fix the right margin at 78 characters.
6. Open the Report Intro Band and add the report title PERSONAL CHECKBOOK. Center the title.
7. Switch the positions of the Page Header Band and the Report Intro Band by selecting Page heading in report intro in the Bands menu.
8. View the report on the screen.
9. Save the report format as CHECKRPT.
10. Print the CHECKRPT report.
11. Close all files.

B: Lesson 7

These projects will demonstrate that a well-written program can be adapted to many applications.

Create a program to append, edit, browse, delete records, and print a report for the CHECKBK file. You will use the program that you created in Lesson 7 by copying it to another program and making changes to the new program.

1. On the DOS util screen, copy ACCOUNTS.PRG to the new name PROJ_2.PRG.
2. Add the PROJ_2 program to the Applications task panel. (Use the Catalog menu and remember to place the highlight in the Applications panel prior to opening the menu.) Use the description "ACCOUNTS PROGRAM MODIFIED FOR PROJECT 2."
3. With the highlight on top of PROJ_2.PRG, press **[Enter]** and select Modify application to enter the program editor.
4. Change the following:
    A. Change the name of the program in the Documentation Section.
    B. Change the name of the database in the Program Environment to A:CHECKBK.DBF.

       C.   Change the label command in the Print Labels Module so that it will print a report instead by changing it to REPORT FORM A:CHECKRPT TO PRINT. Also change the menu choice number 5 to say "PRINT REPORT" instead of PRINT LABELS.

5.   Save these changes.

6.   Run PROJ_2.PRG.

7.   Add three records.

8.   Edit all of the records.

9.   Using Browse or Edit mode, mark one record for deletion.

10.   Pack the database file to erase the marked record.

11.   Print a report.

12.   Return to the DOS prompt.

APPENDIX
C: Civic Club Project

C: Lesson 1

The Civic Club Project creates a database for a civic club. The file contains fields for the name, address, city, state, and zip code of each of its members. The date that each member's dues expire along with the amount of the dues are recorded in the DUES_EXP and DUES_AMT fields. The committee field stores a character that represents the committee that each member serves on. M represents the membership committee, P represents the program committee, and R represents the refreshments committee.

1.   Create a database using the record structure given in Table C-1 below. Name the database file CLUB.

Field Number	Field Name	Field Type	Width	Dec	Index
1	NAME	C	20		N
2	ADDRESS	C	20		N
3	CITY	C	10		N
4	STATE	C	2		N
5	ZIP_CODE	C	10		N
6	DUES_EXP	D	8		N
7	DUES_AMT	N	5	2	N
8	COMMITTEE	C	1		N

Table C-1

2. Print the record structure for the CLUB file.
3. Add the 10 records listed in Table C-2 to the CLUB file.
4. Display the 10 records in CLUB in either Browse or Edit mode.
5. Make a back-up copy of CLUB and verify that the copy was successfully executed.
6. Add the back-up copy of CLUB to the catalog.
7. Close all files.

NAME	ADDRESS	CITY	STATE	ZIP	DUES EXPIRE	DUES AMT	COMMITTEE
ELEONORE HAMMONDS	3605 CRENSHAW	CLOVIS	NM	88101-2958	06/30/93	50.00	P
CHRIS ISHAM	1010 AXTELL	CLOVIS	NM	88101-1890	06/30/93	50.00	R
HELEN GREEN	2397 WEST RIVER ST.	PORTALES	NM	88130-5543	07/31/93	50.00	P
PHYLLIS EISENHOWER	243 AVENUE A	PORTALES	NM	88130-3489	07/31/93	50.00	M
ANN GILBERTSON	1023 BEND DR.	TEXACO	NM	88120-8912	08/31/93	50.00	M
JASON LARSON	98 ROLLINS BLVD.	CLOVIS	NM	88101-1168	08/31/93	50.00	R
BUDDY BILLINGSWORTH	59072 CLOVER POINT	FARWELL	TX	80341-9865	09/30/93	50.00	P
ROY LEE	658 PADUCAH WAY	PADUCAH	TX	80678-9828	09/30/93	50.00	R
RUSTY ALLCOT	708 SW 49TH ST.	CLOVIS	NM	88101-6519	10/31/93	50.00	P
JENNIFER WESTALL	1200 SHERIDAN	PORTALES	NM	88130-6519	10/31/93	50.00	M

Table C-2

C: Lesson 2

Perform the following operations:

1. Open the database file CLUB.
2. Modify the record structure of CLUB by adding a memo field called COMMENTS. Change the width of the NAME field from 20 characters to 25 characters. Print a copy of the new record structure.
3. On the Edit or Browse screen add the following memo notations:
Record 2: CHAIRPERSON OF THE REFRESHMENT COMMITTEE.
Record 4: PAST PRESIDENT OF THE CLUB.

Record 8: FORMER CHAIRPERSON OF THE REFRESHMENT COMMITTEE.

4. Position the record pointer at record 7. Change the contents of the NAME field to: ROY LEE DILLINGHAM, JR.
5. Display all records in the CLUB file.
6. Mark the "JASON LARSON" record for deletion.
7. Erase the marked record.
8. Mark "HELEN GREEN" for deletion.
9. Clear the deletion mark from "HELEN GREEN."
10. Close the CLUB file.

C: Lesson 3

Perform the following operations:

1. Open the CLUB file.
2. Create a query based on CLUB. Set the criterion to include members of the Program committee. View the result.
3. Change the query to set the criterion to include all members of either the Program committee or the Membership committee. View the result.
4. Change the query to set the criterion to include members whose dues expire before September 1, 1993. View the result.
5. Change the query to set the criterion to include all members whose ZIP_CODE begins with the digits 881. Remove all fields from the View skeleton and include only the name, city, state, zip code, and committee fields. View the result.
6. Change the query to set the criterion to include any member with the word CHAIRPERSON in the COMMENTS field. Recall that memo fields can only be queried by using the Condition Box. Add the COMMENTS field to the view. View the result.
7. Save the query with the name CHAIRPER.
8. Close all files.

C: Lesson 4

Perform the following operations:

1. Open the CLUB file.
2. Sort the CLUB file into alphabetical order by CITY. Name the sorted file CLUB1SRT.
3. Display all of the records in CLUB1SRT in Browse mode.
4. Sort the CLUB file by CITY and STATE. Name the sorted file CLUB2SRT.
5. Display all of the records in CLUB2SRT.
6. Make a back-up copy of CLUB2SRT and verify that the copy was successfully executed. Add the back-up copy of CLUB2SRT to the catalog.

7. Create an index for CLUB based on the NAME field and name the index NAME. View the data in Browse mode to check that the index was correctly executed.

8. Create an index for CLUB based on the ZIP_CODE field and name the index ZIP. View the data in Browse mode to check that the index was correctly executed.

9. Switch back to the NAME index and view the data.

10. Switch to Natural Order and view the data.

11. Create an index for CLUB based on COMMITTEE and NAME simultaneously and name the index COMMITTEE. View the data.

12. Add the following record to the CLUB file:
    NAME: POLLY KINNEY
    ADDRESS: 5679 WEST 3RD AVENUE
    CITY: NEW YORK
    STATE: NY
    ZIP CODE: 10935-1111
    DUES EXPIRE: 10/31/93
    DUES AMOUNT: 50.00
    COMMITTEE: P

13. View the data in Browse mode to check that the index correctly placed the new record.

14. Close all files.

C: Lesson 5

Perform the following operations:

1. Open the database file CLUB.

2. Use Browse mode to add the following two records to the CLUB file.
    NAME: MIKE SCHMIDT
    ADDRESS: 404 PLAINS
    CITY: CLOVIS
    STATE: NM
    ZIP CODE: 88101-9812
    DUES EXP: 11/31/93
    DUES AMT: 50.00
    COMMITTEE: P
    NAME: SALLY WESTALL
    ADDRESS: 505 JANEWAY
    CITY: CLOVIS
    STATE: NM
    ZIP CODE: 88101-8412
    DUES EXP: 11/31/93
    DUES AMT: 50.00
    COMMITTEE: M

3. Use Browse mode to change the name BUDDY BILLINGSWORTH to BUDDY HOLLINGSWORTH.

4.   Create a query to mark for deletion all members whose dues expire before 08/01/93. Perform the update, but do NOT erase the marked records.

5.   View the database on the Browse screen and check for the Del denoting the marked records in the Status Bar.

6.   Use the "Unmark all records" selection in the Organize menu on the Browse screen to unmark all records.

7.   Use a Replace query to change "PORTALES" to "PIRTALES" in the CITY field. View the new data.

8.   Use a Replace query to change the dues amount of each member whose dues expire after 09/30/93 to $55.00. Examine the new data.

9.   Save the query as NEW_DUES.

10.   Close all files.

C: Lesson 6

Perform the following operations:

1.   Create a Form report for CLUB. Use a Quick layout to get started.

2.   Move down to the line for the COMMENTS field, press the **[End]** key to jump to the end of that line, and insert two blank lines below the COMMENTS field.

3.   On the second of the two blank lines, draw a single line from the left margin to about 70 on the ruler.

4.   Fix the right margin at 78 characters.

5.   Open the Report Intro Band and add the report title CLUB ROSTER. Center the title.

6.   Switch the positions of the Page Header Band and the Report Intro Band by selecting Page heading in report intro in the Bands menu.

7.   View the report on the screen.

8.   Save the report format as ROSTER.

9.   Print the ROSTER report.

10.   Create a mailing label design for CLUB. Place NAME, ADDRESS, CITY, STATE, and ZIP_CODE in the appropriate places on the label design. Be sure to include a comma after the city name.

11.   View the labels on the screen.

12.   Add the COMMITTEE field at the far right end of the name line.

13.   View the labels on the screen.

14.   Save the label design as MEMBRSHP.

15.   Print the labels.

16.   Close all files.

C: Lesson 7

These projects will demonstrate that a well-written program can be adapted to many applications.

Create a program to append, edit, browse, delete records, and print a report for the CLUB file. You will use the program that you created in Lesson 7 by copying it to another program and making changes to the new program.

1.   On the DOS util screen, copy ACCOUNTS.PRG to the new name PROJ_3.PRG.
2.   Add the PROJ_3 program to the Applications task panel. (Use the Catalog menu and remember to place the highlight in the Applications panel prior to opening the menu.) Use the description "ACCOUNTS PROGRAM MODIFIED FOR PROJECT 3."
3.   With the highlight on top of PROJ_3.PRG, press **[Enter]** and select Modify application to enter the program editor.
4.   Change the following:
       A.   Change the name of the program in the Documentation Section.
       B.   Change the name of the database in the Program Environment to A:CLUB.DBF.
       C.   Change the label command in the Print Labels Module so that it will print a report instead by changing it to REPORT FORM A:ROSTER TO PRINT. Also change the menu choice number 5 to say "PRINT REPORT" instead of PRINT LABELS.
6.   Save these changes.
7.   Run PROJ_3.PRG.
8.   Add three records.
9.   Edit all the records.
10.   Using Browse or Edit mode, mark one record for deletion.
11.   Pack the database file.
12.   Print a report.
13.   Return to DOS.

APPENDIX
D: Personnel Project

D: Lesson 1

The Personnel Project creates a personnel database file for a small business. In addition to entering an employee number and name, each record contains a sales region field, a date of hire, and an annual base salary. The commission field contains a Y for yes or an N for no, to indicate whether or not the employee earns a commission in addition to the base salary.

1. Create a database using the record structure given in Table D-1 below. Name the database file EMPLOYEE.

Field Number	Field Name	Field Type	Width	Dec	Index
1	EMPLOY_NUM	N	9	0	N
2	NAME	C	20		N
3	SALES_REGN	C	5		N
4	HIRE_DATE	D	8		N
5	SALARY	N	10	2	N
6	COMMISSION	C	1		N

Table D-1

2. Print the record structure for the EMPLOYEE file.
3. Add the 10 records listed in Table D-2 to the EMPLOYEE file.
4. Display the 10 records in EMPLOYEE in Browse mode.
5. Make a back-up copy of EMPLOYEE and verify that the copy was successfully executed.

6.   Add the back-up copy to the catalog.
7.   Close the EMPLOYEE file.

EMPLOYEE NUMBER	NAME	SALES REGION	HIRE DATE	SALARY	COMM
983472314	ALVIN BROWNWOOD	SOUTH	07/01/79	35,000.00	N
348547812	RALPH HAMMONDS	EAST	03/31/83	25,000.00	Y
921450923	ALICE BRENTWOOD	NORTH	10/15/83	32,000.00	Y
654236723	SALLY WALKER	SOUTH	02/01/84	15,000.00	N
987234590	HARRY SMITH	WEST	12/03/85	28,000.00	Y
765915195	DONNA NELSON	WEST	12/10/85	28,000.00	Y
435549012	ERIC LARSON	NORTH	04/13/86	30,000.00	Y
982670135	EMILY KINNEY	EAST	05/23/88	40,000.00	N
234475721	ADAM WESTFALL	NORTH	09/17/90	18,000.00	N
447897047	CHRISTOPHER BLACK	SOUTH	11/17/91	26,500.00	Y

Table D-1

D: Lesson 2

Perform the following operations:

1.   Open the database file EMPLOYEE.
2.   Change the width of the NAME field from 20 characters to 25 characters. Print a copy of the new record structure.
3.   Position the record pointer at record 10. Change the NAME to: CHRISTOPHER J. BLACKET.
4.   Move to the EMPLOY_NUM field and search for number 654236723. Change the SALES_REGN to WEST.
5.   Display all records in the EMPLOYEE file.
6.   Mark HARRY SMITH's record for deletion.
7.   Erase the marked record.
8.   Mark the "982670135" record for deletion.
9.   Clear the deletion mark from "982670135."
10.   Make a back-up copy of EMPLOYEE and verify that the copy was successfully executed. Add the back-up copy to the catalog.

11.   Close all files.

D: Lesson 3
Perform the following operations:

1.   Open the database file EMPLOYEE.
2.   Create a query based on EMPLOYEE. Set the criterion to include all items in the SOUTH region. View the result.
3.   Change the query to set the criterion to include all employees with a salary below $30,000.00. View the result.
4.   Change the query to set the criterion to include all employees hired after 1985. View the result.
5.   Change the query to set the criterion to include all employees in the SOUTH sales region who earn more than $20,000.00. Remove all fields from the View skeleton and include only the name and salary fields. View the result.
6.   Change the query to set the criterion to include all employees who are on commission or are in the SOUTH sales region. View the result.
7.   Save the query as SOUTHCOM.
8.   Close all files.

D: Lesson 4
Perform the following operations:

1.   Open the database file EMPLOYEE.
2.   Sort the EMPLOYEE file into alphabetical order by SALES_REGN. Name the sorted file EMP1SRT.
3.   Display all of the records in EMP1SRT.
4.   Sort the EMPLOYEE file by SALES_REGN and HIRE_DATE. Name the sorted file EMP2SRT.
5.   Display all of the records in EMP2SRT.
6.   Make a back-up copy of EMP2SRT. Verify that the copy was successfully executed. Add the back-up copy to the catalog.
7.   Create an index on the EMPLOYEE file based on SALES_REGN and name the index SALES_REGN.
8.   Create an index on the EMPLOYEE file based on EMPLOY_NUM and name the index EMPLOY_NUM.
9.   Switch back to the SALES_REGN index and view the data.
10.   Add the following record to the EMPLOYEE file:
EMPLOYEE NUMBER: 447924089
NAME: JAMES TURNER
SALES_REGN: EAST
HIRE_DATE: 11/17/89
SALARY: 35,000.00
COMMISSION: Y

11. View the data in Browse mode to check that the index correctly placed the new record.
12. Close all files.

D: Lesson 5

Perform the following operations:

1. Open the database file EMPLOYEE.
2. Use Browse mode to add the following two records to the EMPLOYEE file.
   EMPLOY_NUM: 894210999
   NAME: DONNA CARNDUFF
   SALES_REGN: EAST
   HIRE_DATE: 01/05/92
   SALARY: 25,000.00
   COMMISSION: Y
   EMPLOY_NUM:901237891
   NAME: CAROLYN TEAQUE
   SALES_REGN: WEST
   HIRE_DATE: 01/05/92
   SALARY: 25,000.00
   COMMISSION: Y
3. In Browse mode change the NAME for record 7 from ERIC LARSON to ERIC LARSEN.
4. Create a query to mark all employees in the SOUTH region for deletion. Perform the update, but do NOT erase the marked records.
5. View the database on the Browse screen and check for the Del denoting the marked records in the Status Bar.
6. Use the "Unmark all records" selection in the Organize menu on the Browse screen to unmark all records.
7. Use a Replace query to change SOUTH to NORTH in the SALES_REGN field. View the new data.
8. Abandon the query without saving it.
9. Close all files.

D: Lesson 6

Perform the following operations:

1. Create a Column report for EMPLOYEE. Use a Quick layout to get started.
2. Move to the line containing the labels for the column headings (EMPLOY_NUM, NAME, etc.), press the **[End]** key to jump to the end of the line, and backspace over the "MISSION" leaving only the first three letters of COMMISSION.
3. Erase the SUM of the EMPLOY_NUM field in the Report Summary Band.

4. Add a blank line above the remaining sum in the Report Summary Band and draw a line above the sum.
5. Fix the right margin at 78 characters.
6. Open the Report Intro Band and add the report title EMPLOYEE COMMISSION LIST. Center the title.
7. Switch the positions of the Page Header Band and the Report Intro Band by selecting Page heading in report intro in the Bands menu.
8. View the report on the screen.
9. Save the report format as EMP_RPT.
10. Print the EMP_RPT report.
11. Close all files.

D: Lesson 7

These projects will demonstrate that a well-written program can be adapted to many applications.

Create a program to append, edit, browse, delete records, and print a report for the EMPLOYEE file. You will use the program that you created in Lesson 7 by copying it to another program and making changes to the new program.

1. On the DOS util screen, copy ACCOUNTS.PRG to the new name PROJ_4.PRG.
2. Add the PROJ_4 program to the Applications task panel. (Use the Catalog menu and remember to place the highlight in the Applications panel prior to opening the menu.) Use the description "ACCOUNTS PROGRAM MODIFIED FOR PROJECT 4."
3. With the highlight on top of PROJ_4.PRG, press **[Enter]** and select Modify application to enter the program editor.
4. Change the following:
    A. Change the name of the program in the Documentation Section.
    B. Change the name of the database in the Program Environment to A:EMPLOYEE.DBF.
    C. Change the label command in the Print Labels Module so that it will print a report instead by changing it to REPORT FORM A:EMP_RPT TO PRINT. Also change the menu choice number 5 to say "PRINT REPORT" instead of PRINT LABELS.
5. Save these changes.
6. Run PROJ_4.PRG.
7. Add three records.
8. Edit all of the records.
9. Using the Browse or Edit option, mark one record for deletion.
10. Pack the database file.
11. Print a report.
12. Return to DOS.

INDEX

.DBT Extension, 32
.MDX Extension, 59
?, 108
@ R1,C1 TO RZ,CZ DOUBLE, 104
@SAY, 105, 107-109

Abandon Operation, 89
ACCOUNTS.PRG, 103, 112
Add Condition Box, 79
Add Field, 93, 94
Add File to Catalog, 44
Add File to Query, 76
Adding a File to the Catalog, 29
AND Query, 56
Append, 20, 37
APPEND, 106
Append Menu, 20
Applications Panel, 101
ARTRAN File, 25, 29, 30, 56, 83, 99
Ascending Order, 59
ASCII Sort, 60
ASSIST Mode, 3-5, 8, 12, 31

Backup, 13, 27
Backward Search, 39
Bands, 83
Bands Menu, 89
Begin Printing, 91, 112
BROWSE, 109
Browse Mode, 23, 35, 37, 39, 41, 51,
  108
Browse Screen, 60, 65
Buttons, 13

CapsLock Key, 15
CASE, 106-109
Catalog, 4
Catalog Menu, 19, 29, 44, 75

Center a Title, 88
Change Description of Highlighted
  File, 19
Change Drive
    Directory, 14
CLEAR, 104, 108
Clear Deletion Mark, 45
CLOSE ALL, 106, 110
Close Database File, 31
Clock Display, 7
Closing a Menu, 5
Command Mode, 5
Comments, 102
Compiling, 110
Condition Menu, 79
Contents, 13
Control Center, 4, 7, 9, 18, 31
Copy, 42
Create New Index, 67
Creating Label Design, 95
Criterion, 53, 54132

Data Panel, 15, 24, 25, 29, 31, 44
Database, 11
    Create, 15
Database Design Screen, 32, 60
Database File
    Close, 24
Database Pointer, 35
DBMS, 1
Decimal Places, 16
Default Drive
    Directory, 14
    Setting, 14
Delete Query, 71
Deleting Records, 42
Descending Order, 59
Designing Report from a Query, 91

Detail Bank, 86
Dialog Box, 20, 32, 55
Dictionary Sort, 60
Dimensions Menu, 96
Display Data, 23
DO CASE, 106
DO WHILE .T., 104
DOS Menu, 14
DOS Utilities, 14, 27, 42
DOS Utilities Screen, 27, 42
Dot Prompt, 6, 6, 8
Draw a Line, 92

EDIT, 107
Edit Mode, 23, 35, 39, 51
Edit Screen, 20, 60, 65
Editing Record Contents, 35
ENDCASE, 110
ENDDO, 104, 110
Enter Records from Keyboard, 20
Erase File from Disk, 75
Erase Marked Records, 46, 74
Exit, 2, 9, 31, 46, 58, 81, 99, 114

Field Definition Menu, 93, 94, 97
Field Masks, 85, 87
Field Name, 16, 18
Field Type, 16
Field Width, 16
Fields, 11
Fields Menu, 87, 93, 94
File Description, 5, 19
File Extension, 18
File Skeleton, 50, 52, 76
Files Menu, 14
Forward Search, 39, 40, 41, 44, 46
Free Form Report, 91
Function Keys, 8

GET, 104, 105, 107-110
GoTo Menu, 35, 39-41, 44, 46, 78
GOTO TOP, 107-109

Hardware Needed, 1
Help Facility, 12

Index, 16, 59, 64, 67
Insert a Line, 111
Insert Blank Line, 87

Labels Panel, 96, 98
Layout Menu, 76, 84, 87, 92
Line, 87, 92

Margin

Left, 88
Right, 88
Mark, 71
Mark a Record for Deletion, 42, 44
Mark for Deletion, 71
MASTER File, 15, 17, 18, 20, 23, 24,
    29, 32-35, 37, 42, 49, 57, 60, 63, 65,
    67, 69, 75, 79, 96, 98, 104
MASTER.DBK, 42
MASTER.TBK, 42
Memo, 36, 38
Memo Field, 32
Memo Fields, 79
Menu Bar, 4
Message Line, 5
Modify Ruler, 88
Modify Structure/Order, 20
Modifying the Structure, 32
Modules, 106
Multiple Criteria, 56

Natural Order, 69
Navigation Line, 5, 61

Operation Menu, 27, 42
OR Query, 56, 57
Order Records by Index, 69
Organize Menu, 46, 60, 63, 67, 69, 74

Pack, 46, 74
PACK, 108
Packing, 42
Page Footer, 86
Page Header, 86
Page Header Band, 89
Page Heading in Report Intro, 89
Perform the Update, 72, 77
Picklist, 60, 93, 94, 97
PICTURE, 105
Placing a Calculated Field on the
    Report, 93
Placing a Field, 97
Pop-up Menu, 5
Position, 89
Predefined Size, 96
Print, 13
Print a Report, 91
Printing Labels, 98
Print Menu, 86, 90, 93, 94, 97, 112
Print Record Structure, 34
Program Documentation, 102
Program Editor, 101
Program Environment, 103
Program Error Messages, 111
Program Segments, 106

Programming, 101
Programming Commands, 3
Pull-down Menu, 5, 7

Queries Panel, 49, 55, 76, 91, 99
Query, 49
Query by Example, 49
Quick Layout, 84, 91
Quit to DOS, 99

RANGE, 105
READ, 106-110
Record, 11
Record Number, 41
Record Pointer, 42, 44
Record Structure, 12, 15, 17, 25
Records Menu, 44, 45
Related Topics, 13
Remove a File from Catalog, 75
Remove Field, 87
Remove Highlighted File from
  Catalog, 75
Remove Line, 92
Replace, 76
Replace Query, 75
Report
    Add a Field, 93
    Column Layout, 83
    Draw a Line, 87, 92
    Form Layout, 83
    Mail Merge Layout, 83
REPORT FORM TO PRINT, 109
Report Intro Band, 86, 87, 89
Report Summary Band, 86, 87
Reports, 83
Reports Panel, 84, 91, 98
Retrieving a File, 31
RETURN, 106, 110
Ruler, 88, 93
Running dBASE IV, 3

SAY, 104
Searching to Locate a Record, 39
Select Text, 88
Select Update Operation, 71, 76
SET Commands
    SET BELL OFF, 103
    SET BELL ON, 106
    SET CONFIRM OFF, 107-109
    SET CONFIRM ON, 104, 107-110
    SET ESCAPE OFF, 104
    SET STATUS OFF, 103
    SET TALK OFF, 103, 108
    SET TALK ON, 106, 108
Sort, 59, 60

Sort Database on Field List, 60, 63
Status Bar, 7, 15, 23, 26, 36, 38, 44,
    50, 55, 74, 94, 95, 104
Status Line 41, 87
STORE, 105, 107-109
Student Data Disk, 2, 3
Submenu, 7
Switching Indexes, 69

Tag, 66
Task Panels, 5
Tools Menu, 14, 27, 42
Top Record, 44
Transfer to Query Design, 51
Trimming, 97
Two Up, 96

Unmark, 74
Unmark a Record, 45
Untitled.CAT, 15
Update Menu, 71, 72, 76, 77
Update Query, 75
USE MASTER, 104

Variable, 105, 107, 108
Versions, 2
View, 49, 50, 52
View Report on Screen, 86, 90, 93, 94,
    97
View Skeleton, 71, 76

WITH, 76
Words Menu, 88, 89, 92